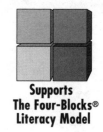

**Supports
The Four-Blocks®
Literacy Model**

Prefixes and Suffixes:
Systematic Sequential Phonics
and Spelling

by
Patricia Cunningham

Editor	Cover Design
Joey Bland	Jennifer Collins

Prefixes and Suffixes
Table of Contents

Prefixes and Suffixes
Introduction

The phonics and spelling challenge for children in the early grades is to learn the beginning letter and rhyming patterns used to spell thousands of words. Children who can read and spell the words **back** and **black** and who know beginning sounds are able to decode and spell numerous rhyming words including **stack**, **snack**, **track**, **crack**, and **shack**. They can also combine rhyming patterns to decode and spell longer words such as **haystack**, **icepack**, and **attack**. By the end of second grade, most children have learned the beginning letter and rhyming patterns from which they can decode and spell thousands of words. (Learning these patterns is the focus of the 140 lessons in *Systematic Sequential Phonics They Use*.)

As children move into third grade and beyond, the new words they encounter are longer. Many of the longer words contain patterns not found in small words. Words such as **dangerous**, **funnier**, and **unhappily** appear difficult to children and cannot be decoded or spelled using beginning letter/ rhyme strategies. Decoding and spelling longer words is also based on patterns but the patterns are not beginning letters and rhymes. The patterns needed for longer words are prefixes, suffixes, and the spelling changes that often accompany the addition of some suffixes. *Prefixes & Suffixes* contains 120 lessons designed to teach these important patterns.

In order to be good readers, children must learn over 100 beginning letter/rhyme patterns. The number of prefixes, suffixes, and spelling changes that must be learned is relatively small. Four prefixes—**re**, **dis**, **un**, and **in/im**—account for over half of all the prefixes readers will ever see. The most common suffixes—**s/es**, **ed**, and **ing**—account for 65 percent of all words with suffixes. Learning other common suffixes such as **en**, **ly**, **er/or**, **tion/sion**, **able/ible**, **al**, **ness**, **er/est**, and **ful/less** allows you to decode and spell thousands of words with suffixes. When suffixes are added to some words, the spelling of the root words changes slightly. Some consonant letters get doubled, **e**'s get dropped, and **y**'s change to **i**'s. While confusing to many children, these spelling changes are relatively few and quite consistent and predictable.

The Lessons

This book contains 120 lessons which teach all the most common prefixes, suffixes, and spelling changes. The lessons are arranged in five-lesson cycles. The first four lessons in each cycle are Making Words lessons. The secret word that ends each Making Words lesson is a key word for one of the prefix, suffix, or spelling change patterns. The fifth lesson in each cycle is a Word Wall lesson in which five words are added to the word wall. These words include words with prefixes or suffixes and some commonly misspelled words. The most common compound words and contractions are also included on the word wall.

Following the 120 lessons are some Review and Extension Activities. These can be used for additional practice as the lessons are being done, as well as when all the lessons are completed. In addition to providing practice with the word wall words, these activities extend the instruction so that students see how the prefixes, suffixes, and spelling changes they have learned can help them read and spell hundreds of other words.

4

The Scope and Sequence

All the most common prefixes, suffixes, and spelling changes are taught and practiced in this program. In addition to learning to decode and spell words with these prefixes and suffixes, students learn how these prefixes and suffixes change the meanings of words and how these words are used in sentences. The most common compounds and contractions are also taught.

Suffixes and Spelling Changes

s/es: **S** is added to words to make them plural or to make verbs agree with nouns. If the root word ends in **s**, **sh**, **ch**, **x**, or **z**, an **es** is added to make the word pronounceable. Normally you can hear when **es** needs to be added after these letters. If the root words ends in **y** with no other vowel ahead of it, the **y** changes to an **i** and **es** is added. The key words are **addresses**, **crashes**, **lunches**, **monkeys**, and **countries**.

ing/ed: **Ing** and **ed** are added to verbs to change how they are used in sentences. If the root word ends in a single consonant and the single consonant follows a single vowel, that consonant is doubled. If the root word ends in an **e**, that **e** is dropped. The key words are **stopping**, **swimming**, **watching**, **writing**, **floated**, **grabbed**, **squirted**, **wanted**, **used**, **fried**, and **married**.

en: **En** is added to words to change how they are used in sentences. If the root word ends in a single consonant and the single consonant follows a single vowel, that consonant is doubled. If the root word ends in an **e**, that **e** is dropped. The key words are **broken**, **frighten**, **hidden**, and **written**.

y: When **y** is added to words, they often become adjectives. If the root word ends in a single consonant and the single consonant follows a single vowel, that consonant is doubled. The key words are **healthy** and **rainy**.

al: When **al** is added to words, they often become adjectives. The key words are **musical** and **national**.

er/est: **Er** and **est** add the meaning of "more" and "most" to words. All the spelling changes of consonant doubling, **e** dropping and **y** changing to **i** apply. The key words are **easiest**, **hardest**, **faster**, **heavier**, **biggest**, **smallest**, **funnier**, and **thinner**.

er/or: **Er** and **or** are often added to verbs to indicate the person or thing that does the action. Consonants are doubled and **e**'s are dropped when **er** or **or** are added. The key words are **computers**, **skater**, **teacher**, **winners**, **builder**, **editor**, **elevator**, **governors**, and **sailor**.

ian/ist/ee: These three suffixes are commonly added to words and indicate people who do things. The key words are **librarian**, **magicians**, **employees**, and **scientist**.

ly: **Ly** is commonly added to words to change them into adverbs. The key words are **brightly**, **friendly**, **probably**, and **really**.

ful/less: The suffixes **ful** and **less** add positive or negative meanings to words. The key words are **beautiful**, **careful**, **helpless**, and **weightless**.

ness: The suffix **ness** changes adjectives into nouns. **Y** changes to **i** when **ness** is added. The key words are **darkness**, **happiness**, **readiness**, and **sadness**.

tion/sion: The suffixes **tion** and **sion** are added to verbs and change the verbs into nouns. All spelling changes apply and words that end in **de** drop the **de** before adding **sion**. The key words are **action**, **inventions**, **location**, **protection**, **vacations**, **confusion**, **discussion**, **decision**, and **explosion**.

able/ible: The suffixes **able** and **ible** often add the meaning of "able to" to words. Key words are **dependable**, **washable**, **sensible**, and **terrible**.

ment: Ment is commonly added to words and turns those words into nouns. Key words are **enjoyment**, **excitement**, **investment**, and **treatment**.

ous: Ous is a suffix that turns words into adjectives. Key words are **dangerous** and **poisonous**.

ic: Ic is another suffix that turns words into adjectives. Key words are **athletic** and **fantastic**.

Prefixes

re: When **re** is added to words, it often adds the meaning of "back" or "again." Key words are **rebuild**, **refilled**, **replace**, and **recalled**.

un: When **un** is added to words, it often adds the meaning of "not" or changes the word into its opposite. Key words are **unbeaten** and **unexpected**.

dis: Dis is another prefix which adds the meaning of "not" or changes the word into its opposite. Key words are **disagree** and **disappear**.

in/im: The prefix **in** (spelled **im** when the root word begins with **m** or **p**, **il** when the root word begins with **l**, and **ir** when the root word begins with **r**) also adds the meaning of "not" or changes the word into its opposite. Key words are **immature**, **impossible**, **incorrect**, and **incomplete**.

Compounds and contractions

The most common compounds and contractions are taught and students learn to spell many other compounds and contractions based on these. The key words are: **anybody**, **anywhere**, **everyone**, **something**, **don't**, **doesn't**, **shouldn't**, **wouldn't**, and **they're**.

Making Words Lessons

Making Words lessons are hands-on, minds-on manipulative activities through which students discover how our English spelling system works. The students are given letters and use these letters to make words as directed by the teacher or tutor. In *Prefixes & Suffixes*, students are handed a letter strip containing all the letters needed for the lesson. After writing the capital letters on the back, they cut the strip into letters and use them to make words. (Reproducible letter strips are found on pages 169-192.)

The order in which students make words is planned to maximize the opportunities for them to discover patterns. In Lesson 58, for example, students begin by making **go**, **goes**, **gone**, and **soon**. Next they make **nose** and are directed to change one letter and spell **rose**. Next, they are asked to move the letters around and spell **sore**. They add a letter to **sore** to spell **snore**. They then make **sooner** and **govern**. The secret word, **governors**, is related to the root word **govern**.

Once the 10-12 words are made, the Sort step of the lesson begins. The words are displayed on cards. Students read all the words in the order made. In *Prefixes & Suffixes*, related words are sorted first. Related words are words that have a common root word. In the **governors** lesson, the related words are:

soon	go	govern
sooner	goes	governors
	gone	

Once related words are sorted, the second sort is for rhyming words.

| nose | sore |
| rose | snore |

The final step of a Making Words lesson is the Transfer step. Students are asked to spell four words that rhyme with the rhyming words. In this lesson they spell **bore**, **store**, **close** and **hose**.

The Making Words lessons in this book are carefully constructed to contain as many related words and rhyming words as possible. In every lesson, students review the important rhyming patterns learned earlier as they learn to look for prefix, suffix, and spelling change patterns. The Making Words lessons are multilevel, providing opportunities for students to focus on the patterns they need to learn.

Because students like to manipulate the letters and come up with their own words, we usually give them a take-home sheet with the same letters used in the lesson. The sheet has the letters across the top and blocks for writing words. Students write capital letters on the back and then cut the letters apart. They manipulate the letters to make words and then write them in the blocks. This is a popular homework assignment with students and their parents. When we write the letters at the top, we write them in alphabetical order–vowels, then consonants–so as not to give away the secret word. Students love being the "smart" ones who "know the secret word," watching parents and other relatives try to figure it out.

Making Words Take-Home Sheet									
e	o	o	g	n	r	r	s	v	

The Word Wall

The word wall is a critical component of *Prefixes and Suffixes*. Five words are added to the word wall in every fifth lesson. These words provide key word examples for all the prefixes, suffixes, and spelling changes along with commonly misspelled words, compound words and contractions. Words are displayed on the wall under the letter of the alphabet with which they begin and in the order introduced in the lessons. (They are not alphabetized by the second letter but are simply placed under the letter with which they begin.)

When words are added to the wall, we discuss the prefixes, suffixes, and spelling changes. We chant the spelling of each word three times to provide an auditory/rhythmic route for retrieving the words. The final activity is writing each word. To make this a bit more interesting, we provide a sentence clue to each word and have students figure out which word fits in the sentence. (Students write only the word–not the sentence.) A reproducible Take-Home Word Wall is given to students each time new words are added. This Take-Home Word Wall can also be used as the only word wall if an individual student is being tutored with this program.

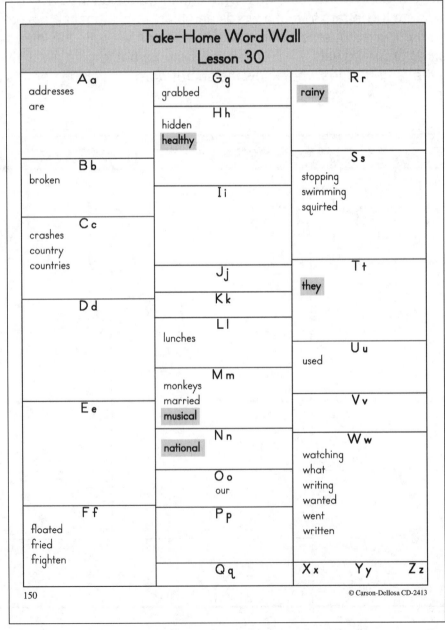

Take-Home Word Wall
Lesson 30

A a	**G g**	**R r**
addresses	grabbed	rainy
are	**H h**	
	hidden	
	healthy	
B b		**S s**
broken		stopping
	I i	swimming
		squirted
C c		
crashes		
country		
countries	**J j**	**T t**
	K k	they
D d	**L l**	
	lunches	
		U u
		used
	M m	
	monkeys	
	married	**V v**
E e	musical	
	N n	**W w**
	national	watching
	O o	what
	our	writing
		wanted
F f	**P p**	went
floated		written
fried		
frighten		
	Q q	**X x** **Y y** **Z z**

150   © Carson-Dellosa CD-2413

After Lesson 5, each lesson contains a Word Wall Review and Extension Activity which help students become automatic at spelling these important words and using these words to spell other words. Here is the list of word wall words and the patterns they represent.

action (tion)
addresses (es)
again (commonly misspelled)
also (commonly misspelled)
anybody (compound)
anywhere (compound)
are (commonly misspelled)
around (commonly misspelled)
athletic (ic, drop e)
beautiful (ful, y-i)
biggest (est, doubling)
brightly (ly)
broken (en, drop e)
builder (er)
careful (ful)
computers (er, drop e)
confusion (sion, drop e)
countries (es, y-i)
country (commonly misspelled)
cousin (commonly misspelled)
crashes (es)
dangerous (ous)
darkness (ness)
decision (sion, d-s, drop e)
dependable (able)
disagree (dis)
disappear (dis)
discussion (sion)
doesn't (contraction)
don't (contraction)
easiest (est, y-i)
editor (or)
elevator (or, drop e)
employees (ee)
enjoyment (ment)
everyone (compound)
except (commonly misspelled)
excitement (ment)
explosion (sion, d-s, drop e)
fantastic (ic)
faster (er)

floated (ed)
fried (ed, y-i)
friendly (ly)
frighten (en)
funnier (er, y-i)
governors (or)
grabbed (ed, doubling)
happiness (ness, y-i)
hardest (est)
have (commonly misspelled)
healthy (y)
heavier (er, y-i)
helpless (less)
hidden (en, doubling)
immature (im)
impossible (im)
incomplete (in)
incorrect (in)
into (commonly misspelled)
inventions (tion)
investment (ment)
librarian (ian, y-i)
location (tion, drop e)
lunches (es)
magicians (ian)
married (ed, y-i)
monkeys (s)
musical (al)
national (al)
none (commonly misspelled)
our (commonly misspelled)
poisonous (ous)
probably (ly, drop e)
protection (tion)
rainy (y)
readiness (ness, y-i)
really (ly)
rebuild (re)
recalled (re)
refilled (re)
replace (re)

right (commonly misspelled)
sadness (ness)
said (commonly misspelled)
sailor (or)
scientist (ist)
sensible (ible, drop e)
shouldn't (contraction)
skater (er, drop e)
smallest (est)
something (compound)
squirted (ed)
stopping (ing, doubling)
swimming (ing, doubling)
teacher (er)
terrible (ible)
their (commonly misspelled)
there (commonly misspelled)
they (commonly misspelled)
they're (contraction)
thinner (er, doubling)
treatment (ment)
unbeaten (un)
unexpected (un)
used (ed, drop e)
vacations (tion, drop e)
wanted (ed)
was (commonly misspelled)
washable (able)
watching (ing)
weightless (less)
went (commonly misspelled)
were (commonly misspelled)
what (commonly misspelled)
winners (er, doubling)
with (commonly misspelled)
wouldn't (contraction)
writing (ing, drop e)
written (en, drop e, doubling)

Lessons 1-5
Suffixes: s; es

Lesson 1

Letters: e o k m n s y
Words: my sky men Ken key keys nose money monkey monkeys

Make Words: Distribute the letters and have everyone write the capitals on the back. After each word is made, show the correct spelling. Make sure everyone has each word spelled correctly before doing the next word. Keep the lesson fast paced.

1. Take 2 letters and spell **my**. This is **my** house.

2. Take 3 letters and spell **sky**. There are lots of clouds in the **sky**.

3. Take 3 letters and spell **men**. Boys grow up to become **men**.

4. Change 1 letter and spell **Ken**. I went fishing with my Uncle **Ken**.

5. Change 1 letter and spell **key**. You need a **key** to unlock the door.

6. Add 1 letter and spell **keys**. I lost my **keys**.

7. Start over and use 4 letters to spell **nose**. That dog has a big **nose**.

8. Take 5 letters to spell **money**. I am saving **money** to buy a bike.

9. Add 1 letter and spell **monkey**. The man has a pet **monkey**.

10. Now it's time for the secret word. Take a minute to see if you can figure it out. (After 1 minute, give clues if needed.) There are lots of **monkeys** at the zoo.

Sort: Display the words on cards in the order they were made and have each word read aloud. Have the related words sorted. Then, have the rhyming words sorted.

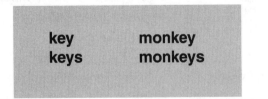

key   monkey
keys   monkeys

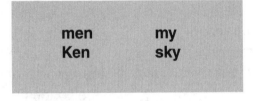

men   my
Ken   sky

Transfer: Say the following words and have everyone use the rhyming words to spell them:

spy ten then try

Lesson 2

Letters: e u c h l n s
Words: us use Sue cue clue hens lens uncle lunch lunches

Make Words: Distribute the letters and have everyone write the capitals on the back. After each word is made, show the correct spelling. Make sure everyone has each word spelled correctly before doing the next word. Keep the lesson fast paced.

1. Take 2 letters and spell **us**. He bought **us** some ice cream.

2. Add 1 letter and spell **use**. Can I **use** your pencil?

3. Move the letters around and spell **Sue**. **Sue** is my sister.

4. Change 1 letter and spell **cue**. When I play the piano, it's your **cue** to start singing.

5. Add 1 letter and spell **clue**. Give me a **clue** so I can guess what's in the box.

6. Start over and use 4 letters to spell **hens**. **Hens** lay eggs.

7. Change 1 letter and spell **lens**. The player's contact **lens** fell out of his eye.

8. Start over and use 5 letters to spell **uncle**. My **uncle** took me to the ball game.

9. Use 5 letters again to spell **lunch**. I am always ready for **lunch**.

10. Now it's time for the secret word. Take a minute to see if you can figure it out. (After 1 minute, give clues if needed.) We packed **lunches** for the picnic.

Sort: Display the words on cards in the order they were made and have each word read aloud. Have the related words sorted. Then, have the rhyming words sorted:

lunch
lunches

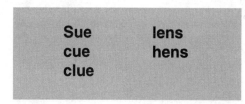

Sue   lens
cue   hens
clue

Transfer: Say the following words and have everyone use the rhyming words to spell them:

true dens pens blue

Lesson 3

Letters: a e c h r s s
Words: are ash cash rash care scare share ashes crash crashes

Make Words: Distribute the letters and have everyone write the capitals on the back. After each word is made, show the correct spelling. Make sure everyone has each word spelled correctly before doing the next word. Keep the lesson fast paced.

1. Take 3 letters and spell **are**. We **are** making words.

2. Take 3 letters and spell **ash**. **Ash** is what is left after wood burns.

3. Add 1 letter and spell **cash**. We went to the bank to **cash** the check.

4. Change 1 letter and spell **rash**. I have a **rash** on my leg and it is very itchy.

5. Start over and use 4 letters to spell **care**. My mom takes **care** of my grandma.

6. Add 1 letter and spell **scare**. Sometimes a loud noise will **scare** you.

7. Change 1 letter and spell **share**. I **share** my snack with my friend.

8. Use 5 letters again to spell **ashes**. We cleaned the **ashes** out of the fireplace.

9. Use 5 letters again to spell **crash**. Ride your bike carefully to avoid a **crash**.

10. Add 2 letters and you can spell the secret word. (Wait 1 minute and then give clues.) There were three **crashes** on this street last month.

Sort: Display the words on cards in the order they were made and have each word read aloud. Have the related words sorted. Then, have the rhyming words sorted.

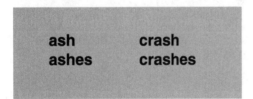

ash	crash
ashes	crashes

ash	care	ashes
rash	scare	crashes
cash	share	
crash		

Transfer: Say the following words and have everyone use the rhyming words to spell them:

smash smashes spare stare

Lesson 4

Letters: a e e d d r s s
Words: sad dad dare dared seeds deeds dress dressed address addresses

Make Words: Distribute the letters and have everyone write the capitals on the back. After each word is made, show the correct spelling. Make sure everyone has each word spelled correctly before doing the next word. Keep the lesson fast paced.

1. Take 3 letters and spell **sad**. I was very **sad** when my cat died.
2. Change 1 letter and spell **dad**. My **dad** said we could get a baby kitten.
3. Take 4 letters and spell **dare**. I **dare** you to do it!
4. Add 1 letter and spell **dared**. My brother **dared** me to jump off the big rock.
5. Start over and use 5 letters to spell **seeds**. We planted apple **seeds**.
6. Change 1 letter and spell **deeds**. In scouts, we earn badges for good **deeds**.
7. Start over and use 5 letters to spell **dress**. The bride wore a beautiful **dress**.
8. Add 2 letters and spell **dressed**. We got **dressed** up for the wedding.
9. Start over and use 7 letters to spell **address**. She wrote the **address** on the envelope.
10. Add 2 letters and you can spell the secret word. (Wait 1 minute and then give clues.) I have lived in three places and had three different **addresses**.

Sort: Display the words on cards in the order they were made and have each word read aloud. Have the related words sorted. Then, have the rhyming words sorted.

dress	address		sad	seeds
dressed	addresses		dad	deeds

Transfer: Say the following words and have everyone use the rhyming words to spell them:

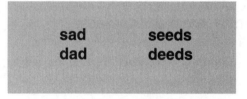

weeds bad glad bleeds

Lesson 5

Word Wall Words: addresses are crashes lunches monkeys
Suffixes for Review: s; es

Give everyone a copy of the first word wall (p. 145) and/or place the words on the classroom word wall.

Review:

Explain that four of the words were the secret words and end in **s** or **es**. The fifth word, **are** is included because it is a word that is often misspelled. Point out that **monkeys** is the word **monkey** with just an **s** added, **lunches**, **crashes**, and **addresses** are **lunch**, **crash**, and **address** with **es** added. If a word ends in **ch**, **sh**, or **s**, the ending we add is **es**.

Word Wall:

Call out the five words one at a time and have everyone chant the spelling three times for each word (for example: "m-o-n-k-e-y-s, monkeys; m-o-n-k-e-y-s, monkeys; m-o-n-k-e-y-s, monkeys;" and "l-u-n-c-h-e-s, lunches; l-u-n-c-h-e-s, lunches; l-u-n-c-h-e-s, lunches"). Next, have everyone write the five words as you give sentence clues.

1. We saw _____ at the zoo.

2. At the end of the movie, a priceless statue almost _____ to the ground.

3. I have lived in four different places and had four different _____.

4. Where _____ our new books?

5. We went on a trip and packed _____ to have a picnic on the way.

Lessons 6-10
Suffix: ing

Lesson 6

Letters: a i c g h n t w
Words: hat cat act what wing thing night watch acting watching

Make Words: Distribute the letters and have everyone write the capitals on the back. After each word is made, show the correct spelling. Make sure everyone has each word spelled correctly before doing the next word. Keep the lesson fast paced.

1. Take 3 letters and spell **hat**. <u>She wore a big **hat**.</u>

2. Change 1 letter and spell **cat**. <u>The mother **cat** had 5 kittens.</u>

3. Move the letters around and spell **act**. <u>I like to **act** in plays.</u>

4. Start over and use 4 letters to spell **what**. <u>**What** do you want to eat?</u>

5. Use 4 letters again to spell **wing**. <u>The mother bird sheltered the baby bird under its **wing**.</u>

6. Take the **w** away and add 2 letters to spell **thing**. <u>What do you call this **thing**?</u>

7. Move the letters around and spell **night**. <u>It gets dark at **night**.</u>

8. Start over and use 5 letters to spell **watch**. <u>I **watch** TV on Saturday mornings.</u>

9. Now, let's make a 6-letter word, **acting**. <u>She was not **acting** right.</u>

10. It's time for the secret word. Use all your letters and spell a word that adds **ing** to a word we already made. (Wait 1 minute and then give clues.) <u>We were **watching** the parade.</u>

Sort: Display the words on cards in the order they were made and have each word read aloud. Have the related words sorted. Then, have the rhyming words sorted.

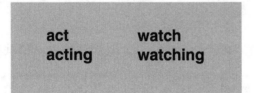

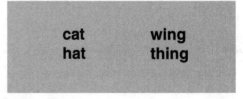

Transfer: Say the following words and have everyone use the rhyming words to spell them.

spring that bring string

Word Wall: Have everyone look at the word wall. Call out the five words and have everyone chant them and write them. Have everyone underline the **es** in **lunches**, **crashes**, and **addresses**.

Lesson 7

Letters: i i g n r t w
Words: win wig twig twin grin ring wing wiring tiring writing

Make Words: Distribute the letters and have everyone write the capitals on the back. After each word is made, show the correct spelling. Make sure everyone has each word spelled correctly before doing the next word. Keep the lesson fast paced.

1. Take 3 letters and spell **win**. <u>I hope my team will **win** the game.</u>
2. Change 1 letter and spell **wig**. <u>The clown wore a green **wig**.</u>
3. Add 1 letter and spell **twig**. <u>A tiny branch is called a **twig**.</u>
4. Change 1 letter and spell **twin**. <u>I wish I had a **twin** brother.</u>
5. Change 2 letters and spell **grin**. <u>The boy who won had a big **grin** on his face.</u>
6. Move the letters around and spell **ring**. <u>We bought my mom a pretty **ring**.</u>
7. Change 1 letter and spell **wing**. <u>The bird could not fly because its **wing** was broken.</u>
8. Take 6 letters and spell **wiring**. <u>They are **wiring** our computer lab so we can use the Internet.</u>
9. Change 1 letter and spell **tiring**. <u>The long car trip was very **tiring**.</u>
10. It's time for the secret word. (Wait 1 minute and then give clues.) <u>I like **writing** stories.</u>

Sort: Display the words on cards in the order they were made and have each word read aloud. Have the rhyming words sorted.

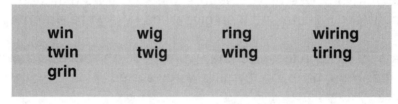

win	wig	ring	wiring
twin	twig	wing	tiring
grin			

Transfer: Say the following words and have everyone use the rhyming words to spell them:

> thing spin firing fig

Word Wall: Have everyone look at the word wall and chant the spelling of each word. Explain that all the words except **are** can be models for spelling other words. Have everyone write the following words using the word wall words as models: **punches, cashes, keys, dresses, bunches**.

Lesson 8

Make Words: Distribute the letters and have everyone write the capitals on the back. After each word is made, show the correct spelling. Make sure everyone has each word spelled correctly before doing the next word. Keep the lesson fast paced.

1. Take 2 letters and spell **in**. We played **in** the house.

2. Add 1 letter and spell **win**. The fastest runner will **win** the race.

3. Change 1 letter and spell **wig**. The lady wore a long blond **wig**.

4. Add 1 letter and spell **wing**. My dog chewed up one **wing** of my model airplane.

5. Change 1 letter and spell **sing**. We **sing** songs on the bus.

6. Move the letters around and spell **sign**. The **sign** says, "No parking."

7. Use 4 letters to spell **swim**. I learned to **swim** when I was five.

8. Use 5 letters to spell **wings**. Eagles have very large **wings**.

9. Move the letters around to spell **swing**. We bought a new **swing** set.

10. It's time for the secret word. I will give you a minute to see if you can figure it out. (After 1 minute, give clues.) We all went **swimming** at the pool.

Sort: Display the words on cards in the order they were made and have each word read aloud. Have the related words sorted. Then, have the rhyming words sorted.

wing	swim		in	wing
wings	swimming		win	sing
				swing

Transfer: Say the following words and have everyone use the rhyming words to spell them:

bring sting grin thin

Word Wall: Have everyone look at the word wall and chant the spelling of each word. Spell some root words ("push, p-u-s-h") and have everyone write each word with the **s** or **es** ending: **pushes, inches, turkeys, bosses, ranches.**

Lesson 9

Letters: i o g n p p s t
Words: top tip pit spit spot song sing sign sting points stopping

Make Words: Distribute the letters and have everyone write the capitals on the back. After each word is made, show the correct spelling. Make sure everyone has each word spelled correctly before doing the next word. Keep the lesson fast paced.

1. Take 3 letters and spell **top**. <u>The candy is on the **top** shelf.</u>
2. Change 1 letter and spell **tip**. <u>If you lose your balance, you will **tip** over.</u>
3. Move the letters around and spell **pit**. <u>A big hole is called a **pit**.</u>
4. Add 1 letter and spell **spit**. <u>I took one swallow of the spoiled milk and **spit** it out.</u>
5. Change 1 letter and spell **spot**. <u>This is the **spot** where we want to plant the tree.</u>
6. Use 4 letters to spell **song**. <u>What is your favorite **song**?</u>
7. Change 1 letter and spell **sing**. <u>Do you like to **sing**?</u>
8. Move the letters around and spell **sign**. <u>My mom had to **sign** the note.</u>
9. Use 5 letters to spell **sting**. <u>A bee can **sting** you.</u>
10. Use 6 letters to spell **points**. <u>Our team won the game by 14 **points**.</u>
11. Can you figure out the secret word? Take a minute and see if you can. (Give clues after 1 minute.) <u>I think the rain is **stopping**.</u>

Sort: Display the words on cards in the order they were made and have each word read aloud. Have the related words sorted. Then, have the rhyming words sorted.

stop
stopping

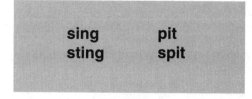

sing   **pit**
sting   **spit**

Transfer: Say the following words and have everyone use the rhyming words to spell them:

cling hit slit sling

Word Wall: Have everyone look at the word wall and chant the spelling of each word. Spell some root words ("tray, t-r-a-y") and have everyone write each word with the **s** or **es** ending: **trays**, **bushes**, **benches**, **enjoys**, **passes**.

Lesson 10

Word Wall Words: stopping swimming watching what writing
Suffix for Review: ing

Give everyone a copy of the word wall (p. 146) and/or place the words on the classroom word wall.

Review:

Notice that four of the words were the secret words and end in **ing**. The fifth word, **what**, is included on the word wall because it is a word that is often misspelled. Point out that **watching** is the word **watch** with just an **ing** added, **stopping** and **swimming** are **stop** and **swim** with the final consonant doubled before adding the **ing**. If a word has one vowel and then a single consonant, we double that consonant before adding endings such as **ing**. When we add **ing** to words that end with **e** such as **write**, we drop the **e**.

Word Wall:

Call out the five words one at a time and have everyone chant the spelling three times for each word (for example: "s-t-o-p-p-i-n-g, stopping; s-t-o-p-p-i-n-g, stopping; s-t-o-p-p-i-n-g, stopping"). Next, have everyone write the five words as you give sentence clues.

1. We were _____ letters to our pen pals.

2. We went _____ at the pool.

3. I don't know _____ kind of ice cream to get.

4. I like _____ TV.

5. The brakes on my bike broke and I had trouble _____.

Lessons 11-15
Suffix: ed

Lesson 11

Letters: a e d n t w
Words: an and ant tan ten den dent went want wanted

Make Words: Distribute the letters and have everyone write the capitals on the back. After each word is made, show the correct spelling. Make sure everyone has each word spelled correctly before doing the next word. Keep the lesson fast paced.

1. Take 2 letters and spell **an**. She ate **an** apple.

2. Take 3 letters and spell **and**. My friend **and** I go swimming at the pool.

3. Change 1 letter and spell **ant**. I watched an **ant** going into the anthill.

4. Move the letters around and spell **tan**. We bought a **tan** van.

5. Change 1 letter and spell **ten**. I have **ten** fingers and **ten** toes.

6. Change 1 letter and spell **den**. They are in the **den** watching TV.

7. Add 1 letter and spell **dent**. She was angry that her new car had a **dent** in it.

8. Change 1 letter and spell **went**. After dinner, we **went** to the mall.

9. Change 1 letter and spell **want**. What do you **want**?

10. It's time for the secret word. Add your letters to want. (Wait 1 minute, then give clues.) I **wanted** to go swimming.

Sort: Display the words on cards in the order they were made and have each word read aloud. Have the related words sorted. Then, have the rhyming words sorted.

want
wanted

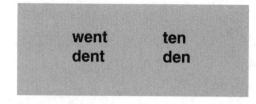

went   ten
dent   den

Transfer: Say the following words and have everyone use the rhyming words to spell them:

bent then when spent

Word Wall: Have everyone look at the word wall. Call out the five new words (**stopping, watching, swimming, want, writing**) and have everyone chant them and write them. Have everyone underline the **ing** in **writing, stopping, swimming,** and **watching**.

Lesson 12

Letters: a e b b d g r
Words: are red bed bad bag rag drag grad grab grade grabbed

Make Words: Distribute the letters and have everyone write the capitals on the back. After each word is made, show the correct spelling. Make sure everyone has each word spelled correctly before doing the next word. Keep the lesson fast paced.

1. Take 3 letters and spell **are**. There **are** lots of people coming to watch the game.

2. Take 3 letters and spell **red**. Strawberries are **red**.

3. Change 1 letter and spell **bed**. It is time to go to **bed**.

4. Change 1 letter and spell **bad**. The opposite of good is **bad**.

5. Change 1 letter and spell **bag**. I put the groceries in the **bag**.

6. Change 1 letter and spell **rag**. I wiped the floor and threw the dirty **rag** in the washer.

7. Add 1 letter and spell **drag**. We had to **drag** the heavy boxes into the garage.

8. Move the letters around and spell **grad**. We call a person who graduates a **grad**.

9. Change 1 letter and spell **grab**. It is not polite to **grab** things.

10. Use 5 letters to spell **grade**. My brother is in fifth **grade**.

11. Add your letters to a word we already made and you will have the secret word. (Give clues after 1 minute.) The baby reached out and **grabbed** by finger.

Sort: Display the words on cards in the order they were made and have each word read aloud. Have the related words sorted. Then, have the rhyming words sorted.

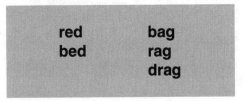

| grab
grabbed | | red
bed | bag
rag
drag |

Transfer: Say the following words and have everyone use the rhyming words to spell them:

brag   bled   shred   wag

Word Wall: Have everyone look at the word wall and chant the spelling of the five new words. Explain that all the new words except **want** can be models for spelling other words. Have everyone spell the following words using the word wall words as models: **popping, biting, catching, trimming, hopping**.

Lesson 13

Letters: e i u d q r s t
Words: it sit use used dirt quit quite quiet squirt squirted

Make Words: Distribute the letters and have everyone write the capitals on the back. After each word is made, show the correct spelling. Make sure everyone has each word spelled correctly before doing the next word. Keep the lesson fast paced.

1. Take 2 letters and spell **it**. <u>Where did you buy **it**?</u>

2. Add 1 letter and spell **sit**. <u>Where do you want to **sit**?</u>

3. Take 3 letters and spell **use**. <u>It's my turn to **use** the computer.</u>

4. Add 1 letter and spell **used**. <u>We bought a **used** car.</u>

5. Take 4 letters and spell **dirt**. <u>My dog likes to eat **dirt**.</u>

6. Use 4 letters again to spell **quit**. <u>Mom asked me to **quit** teasing my sister.</u>

7. Add 1 letter and spell **quite**. <u>I am not **quite** done.</u>

8. Move the letters around and spell **quiet**. <u>Please be **quiet** in the library.</u>

9. Take 6 letters and spell **squirt**. <u>I bought a **squirt** gun.</u>

10. Add your letters to **squirt** and you will have the secret word. (Give clues after 1 minute.)
    <u>I **squirted** my sister and my dog.</u>

Sort: Display the words on cards in the order they were made and have each word read aloud. Have the related words sorted. Then, have the rhyming words sorted.

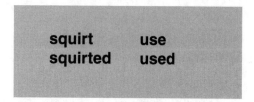

squirt   use
squirted   used

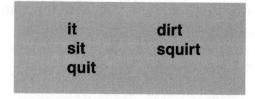

it   dirt
sit   squirt
quit

Transfer: Say the following words and have everyone use the rhyming words to spell them:

shirt skirt grit spit

Word Wall: Have everyone look at the word wall and chant the spelling of each word. Spell some root words ("vote, v-o-t-e") and have everyone spell that word with the **ing** ending: **voting, humming, riding, tripping, fishing.**

Lesson 14

Letters: a e o d f l t
Words: eat ate old fold told toad load date float floated

Make Words: Distribute the letters and have everyone write the capitals on the back. After each word is made, show the correct spelling. Make sure everyone has each word spelled correctly before doing the next word. Keep the lesson fast paced.

1. Take 3 letters and spell **eat**. What do you **eat** for breakfast?

2. Move the letters around and spell **ate**. Yesterday I **ate** pancakes.

3. Take 3 letters and spell **old**. How **old** is your grandma?

4. Add 1 letter and spell **fold**. **Fold** your paper in half.

5. Change 1 letter and spell **told**. My dad **told** me to be home before dark.

6. Change 1 letter and spell **toad**. The **toad** hopped down the sidewalk.

7. Change 1 letter and spell **load**. The truck brought us a **load** of firewood.

8. Use 4 letters again to spell **date**. What is today's **date**?

9. Use 5 letters to spell **float**. Do you know how to **float**?

10. Add your letters to **float** and you will have the secret word. (Give clues after 1 minute.)
We **floated** down the river on a raft.

Sort: Display the words on cards in the order they were made and have each word read aloud. Have the related words sorted. Then, have the rhyming words sorted.

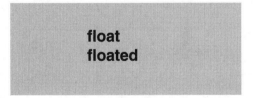

float
floated

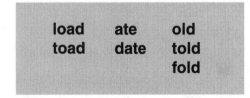

load	ate	old
toad	date	told
		fold

Transfer: Say the following words and have everyone use the rhyming words to spell them:

scold gate road skate

Word Wall: Call out five of the word wall words that need spelling changes before endings are added. Have everyone chant them, write them and tell what spelling changes are needed: **lunches, crashes, writing, swimming, stopping.**

Lesson 15

Word Wall Words: floated grabbed squirted used wanted
Suffix for Review: ed

Give everyone a copy of the word wall (p. 147) and/or place the words on the classroom word wall.

Review:

All five words have the **ed** ending. We double the **b** in **grab** when adding **ed** because **b** is one consonant following one vowel. We don't double the **t** in **float** because there are two vowels before the **t**. We don't double the **t** in **squirt** because **squirt** ends in two consonants, **r** and **t**. **Want** also ends in two consonants, **n** and **t**. **Use** ends with an **e**, so we just add the **d** to have the **ed** ending.

Word Wall:

Call out the five words one at a time and have everyone chant the spelling three times for each word (for example: "u-s-e-d, used; u-s-e-d, used; u-s-e-d, used"). Next, have everyone write the five words as you give sentence clues.

1. The toys _____ in the bathtub.

2. I _____ water on my brother.

3. I got everything I _____ for my birthday.

4. The baby _____ her mother's hand.

5. We _____ tape to hold the sides of the box together.

Lessons 16-20
Suffixes: s; es; d in words ending in y

Lesson 16

Letters: o u c n r t y
Words: cry try our your turn torn corn count county country

Make Words: Distribute the letters and have everyone write the capitals on the back. After each word is made, show the correct spelling. Make sure everyone has each word spelled correctly before doing the next word. Keep the lesson fast paced.

1. Take 3 letters and spell **cry**. When I feel very sad, I **cry**.

2. Change 1 letter and spell **try**. I always **try** to do my best.

3. Use 3 letters to spell **our**. **Our** class is putting on a play.

4. Add 1 letter and spell **your**. Let's play at **your** house today.

5. Use 4 letters to spell **turn**. It is my **turn** to choose the cereal.

6. Change 1 letter and spell **torn**. My favorite jeans are **torn** in several places.

7. Change 1 letter and spell **corn**. I like **corn** on the cob.

8. Use 5 letters to spell **count**. My little brother can **count** to ten.

9. Add 1 letter and spell **county**. My friend lives in Washington **County**.

10. It's time for the secret word. Add 1 letter somewhere to **county** and you will have it. (Wait 1 minute and then give clues.) Our **country** is the United States.

Sort: Display the words on cards in the order they were made and have each word read aloud. Have the rhyming words sorted.

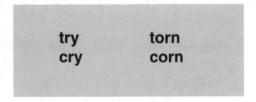

try   torn
cry   corn

Transfer: Say the following words and have everyone use the rhyming words to spell them:

born fly shy spy

Word Wall: Have everyone look at the word wall. Call out the five new words and have everyone chant them and write them. Then, have everyone underline the **ed** in each word: **wanted**, **squirted**, **used**, **grabbed**, **floated**.

Lesson 17

Letters: e i o u c n r t s
Words: our sour turn torn corn count cries tries cousin countries

Make Words: Distribute the letters and have everyone write the capitals on the back. After each word is made, show the correct spelling. Make sure everyone has each word spelled correctly before doing the next word. Keep the lesson fast paced.

1. Take 3 letters and spell **our**. <u>**Our** class is the best class in the school.</u>
2. Add 1 letter and spell **sour**. <u>I thought the lemonade was too **sour**.</u>
3. Use 4 letters to spell **turn**. <u>**Turn** your paper over and draw a picture on the back.</u>
4. Change 1 letter and spell **torn**. <u>My shirt got **torn** when I fell off my bike.</u>
5. Change 1 letter and spell **corn**. <u>**Corn** is my favorite vegetable.</u>
6. Use 5 letters to spell **count**. <u>Please **count** the chairs to see if we have enough.</u>
7. Use 5 letters to spell **cries**. <u>The baby **cries** when she is hungry.</u>
8. Change 1 letter and spell **tries**. <u>My little brother **tries** to do everything I do.</u>
9. Use 6 letters to spell **cousin**. <u>My **cousin** lives in the house next door.</u>
10. It's time for the secret word. (Wait 1 minute and then give clues.) <u>I would like to visit all the **countries** in the world.</u>

Sort: Display the words on cards in the order they were made and have each word read aloud. Have the rhyming words sorted.

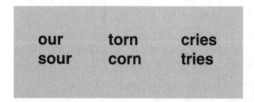

our	torn	cries
sour	corn	tries

Transfer: Say the following words and have everyone use the rhyming words to spell them:

flies flour scour dries

Word Wall: Have everyone look at the word wall and chant the spelling of each word. Spell some root words ("vote, v-o-t-e") and have everyone write each word with the **ed** ending: **voted**, **hummed**, **saved**, **tripped**, **fished**.

Lesson 18

Letters: e i d f r
Words: Ed red fed ref rid ride Fred fire fired fried

Make Words: Distribute the letters and have everyone write the capitals on the back. After each word is made, show the correct spelling. Make sure everyone has each word spelled correctly before doing the next word. Keep the lesson fast paced.

1. Take 2 letters and spell **Ed**. <u>My Uncle **Ed** is coming to visit.</u>

2. Add 1 letter and spell **red**. <u>**Red** is my favorite color.</u>

3. Change 1 letter and spell **fed**. <u>I **fed** the dog.</u>

4. Use 3 letters to spell **ref**. <u>The referee is also called the **ref**.</u>

5. Use 3 letters to spell **rid**. <u>I cleaned out my room and got **rid** of some old toys.</u>

6. Add 1 letter and spell **ride**. <u>Can I **ride** your bike?</u>

7. Use 4 letters and spell **Fred**. <u>My dog's name is **Fred**.</u>

8. Use 4 letters to spell **fire**. <u>The **fire** truck raced down the street.</u>

9. There are 2 secret words today. See if you can figure them out. (After 1 minute, give some clues.) <u>The man was **fired** from his job cooking **fried** chicken.</u>

Sort: Display the words on cards in the order they were made and have each word read aloud. Have the related words sorted. Then, have the rhyming words sorted.

fire
fired

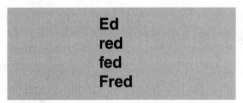

Ed
red
fed
Fred

Transfer: Say the following words and have everyone use the rhyming words to spell them:

sled sped shed shred

Word Wall: Call out five words that don't need any changes when endings are added. Have everyone chant and write the following words: **monkeys**, **floated**, **squirted**, **wanted**, **watching**.

Make Words: Distribute the letters and have everyone write the capitals on the back. After each word is made, show the correct spelling. Make sure everyone has each word spelled correctly before doing the next word. Keep the lesson fast paced.

1. Take 3 letters and spell **red**. He has a **red** truck.

2. Change 1 letter and spell **rid**. We had a yard sale and got **rid** of lots of old stuff.

3. Add 1 letter and spell **ride**. We **ride** to school on the bus.

4. Use 4 letters to spell **read**. I like to **read** books about animals.

5. Move the letters around and spell **dear**. I wrote "**Dear** Grandma" at the beginning of my letter.

6. Move the letters again and spell **dare**. I **dare** you to jump over that puddle.

7. Change 1 letter and spell **rare**. She likes her steaks **rare** but I like mine well done.

8. Move the letters around and spell **rear**. She sat in the **rear** of the boat.

9. Use 5 letters to spell **dream**. I had a wonderful **dream** last night.

10. It's time for the secret word. (Wait 1 minute and then give clues.)
    My cousin is getting **married** next Saturday.

Sort: Display the words on cards in the order they were made and have each word read aloud. Have the rhyming words sorted.

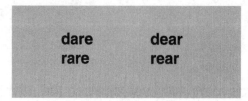

dare	dear
rare	rear

Transfer: Say the following words and have everyone use the rhyming words to spell them:

spare spear fear gear

Word Wall: Call out five of the word wall words that need spelling changes before endings are added. Have everyone chant them, write them, and tell what spelling changes are needed:
lunches, **addresses**, **writing**, **swimming**, **grabbed**.

Lesson 20

Word Wall Words: country countries fried married our
Suffixes for Review: s; es; d in words ending in y

Give everyone a copy of the word wall (p. 148) and/or place the words on the classroom word wall.

Review:

Our is added to the word wall because it is a word that is often misspelled. **Country** and **countries** help us remember that when a word ends in **y**, we change the **y** to **i** and add **es**. The root word for **fried** is **fry**. The root word for **married** is **marry**. The **y** is changed to **i** before the **ed** is added. Explain that we don't change the **y** to **i** if there is another vowel in front of the **y**. **Monkey** ends in **ey** and we just add **s**.

Word Wall:

Call out the five words one at a time and have everyone chant the spelling three times for each word (for example: "f-r-i-e-d, fried; f-r-i-e-d, fried; f-r-i-e-d, fried"). Next, have everyone write the five words as you give sentence clues.

1. I like _____ chicken.

2. I went to the wedding to watch my cousin get _____.

3. The United States is our _____.

4. Mexico and Canada are _____ I would like to visit.

5. Everyone came over to _____ house to play.

Lessons 21-25
Suffix: en

Lesson 21

Letters: e i f g h n r t
Words: hit fit grit ring thing night right fight fright frighten

Make Words: Distribute the letters and have everyone write the capitals on the back. After each word is made, show the correct spelling. Make sure everyone has each word spelled correctly before doing the next word. Keep the lesson fast paced.

1. Take 3 letters and spell **hit**. The batter **hit** a home run.

2. Change 1 letter and spell **fit**. These old shoes don't **fit** any more.

3. Take the **f** off and add 2 letters to spell **grit**. There was a lot of **grit** on the floor of the garage.

4. Use 4 letters to spell **ring**. Did you hear the phone **ring**?

5. Take the **r** off and add two letters to spell **thing**. Do you know what that **thing** is called?

6. Move the letters around and spell **night**. **Night** is the opposite of day.

7. Change 1 letter and spell **right**. I knew all the **right** answers.

8. Change 1 letter and spell **fight**. I try to never get in a **fight**.

9. Add 1 letter and spell **fright**. The loud thunder gave me quite a **fright**.

10. It's time for the secret word. Add your letter to **fright** and see if you can figure it out. (Wait 1 minute and then give clues.) My brother gets mad when I sneak up behind him and **frighten** him.

Sort: Display the words on cards in the order they were made and have each word read aloud. Have the related words sorted. Then, have the rhyming words sorted.

fright		hit	ring	night
frighten		fit	thing	right
		grit		fright
				fight

Transfer: Say the following words and have everyone use the rhyming words to spell them:

flight bright slit fling

Word Wall: Have everyone look at the word wall. Call out the five new words and have everyone chant them and write them: **our, fried, married, country, countries.**

Lesson 22

Letters: e o b k n r
Words: or on Ron Rob Ken Ben born bone broke broken

Make Words: Distribute the letters and have everyone write the capitals on the back. After each word is made, show the correct spelling. Make sure everyone has each word spelled correctly before doing the next word. Keep the lesson fast paced.

1. Take 2 letters and spell **or**. Do you like football **or** basketball better?
2. Change 1 letter and spell **on**. Your lunch money is **on** the table.
3. Add 1 letter and spell **Ron**. **Ron** and I are good friends.
4. Change 1 letter and spell **Rob**. **Rob** is my friend too.
5. Let's spell another name, **Ken**. **Ken** is Rob's brother.
6. Let's spell one more name, **Ben**. **Ben** is Ken's cousin.
7. Use 4 letters to spell **born**. I was **born** in Florida.
8. Use 4 letters to spell **bone**. I gave my dog a big **bone** to chew.
9. Use 5 letters to spell **broke**. My little brother **broke** his favorite toy.
10. It's time for the secret word. (Wait 1 minute and then give clues.)
    The radio doesn't work because it is **broken**.

Sort: Display the words on cards in the order they were made and have each word read aloud. Have the related words sorted. Then, have the rhyming words sorted.

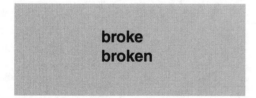

broke
broken

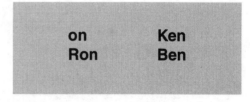

on	Ken
Ron	Ben

Transfer: Say the following words and have everyone use the rhyming words to spell them:

then when con men

Word Wall: Have everyone look at the word wall and chant the spelling of the five new words (**country, countries, our, married, fried**). Have everyone spell the following words using the word wall words as models: **carried, carries, tried, tries, cried.**

Lesson 23

Letters: e i d d h n
Words: Ed end den hen did hid hide dine dined hidden

Make Words: Distribute the letters and have everyone write the capitals on the back. After each word is made, show the correct spelling. Make sure everyone has each word spelled correctly before doing the next word. Keep the lesson fast paced.

1. Take 2 letters and spell **Ed**. I sat next to **Ed** on the bus.
2. Add 1 letter and spell **end**. The movie will **end** at 9:30.
3. Move the letters around and spell **den**. We watch TV in the **den**.
4. Change 1 letter and spell **hen**. I love the story of the Little Red **Hen**.
5. Use 3 letters to spell **did**. **Did** you watch the game last night?
6. Change 1 letter and spell **hid**. I **hid** the gifts I bought for my mom.
7. Add 1 letter and spell **hide**. Sometimes I forget where I **hide** things.
8. Use 4 letters to spell **dine**. My parents like to **dine** at fancy restaurants.
9. Add 1 letter and spell **dined**. After the wedding, we **dined** at The Palace.
10. It's time for the secret word. Use all your letters and spell a word that adds **d-e-n** to a word we already made. (Wait 1 minute and then give clues.) The gifts are **hidden** under the bed.

Sort: Display the words on cards in the order they were made and have each word read aloud. Have the related words sorted. Then, have the rhyming words sorted.

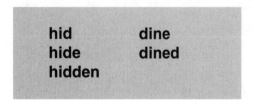

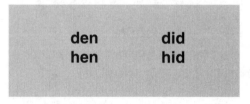

hid	dine
hide	dined
hidden	

| den | did |
| hen | hid |

Transfer: Say the following words and have everyone use the rhyming words to spell them:

skid slid ten then

Word Wall: Call out five of the word wall words without their endings. Have everyone chant and write the following root words: **lunch, float, watch, want, monkey.**

Lesson 24

Letters: e i n r t t w
Words: in win twin went tent rent wire write winter written

Make Words: Distribute the letters and have everyone write the capitals on the back. After each word is made, show the correct spelling. Make sure everyone has each word spelled correctly before doing the next word. Keep the lesson fast paced.

1. Use 2 letters to spell **in**. The opposite of out is **in**.

2. Add 1 letter and spell **win**. I think we will **win** the game.

3. Add 1 letter and spell **twin**. I wish I had a **twin** sister.

4. Use 4 letters to spell **went**. We **went** to see a play.

5. Change 1 letter and spell **tent**. I like camping out in a **tent**.

6. Change 1 letter and spell **rent**. We pay the **rent** for our apartment every month.

7. Use 4 letters to spell **wire**. Be careful you don't trip over the **wire**.

8. Use 5 letters to spell **write**. I like to **write** in my journal.

9. Use 6 letters to spell **winter**. In the **winter**, it snows a lot.

10. It's time for the secret word. (Wait 1 minute and then give clues.) I have **written** three letters to my pen pal.

Sort: Display the words on cards in the order they were made and have each word read aloud. Have the related words sorted. Then, have the rhyming words sorted.

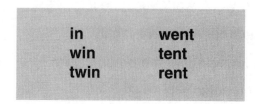

Transfer: Say the following words and have everyone use the rhyming words to spell them:

spent grin chin thin

Word Wall: Call out five of the word wall words that need spelling changes without the endings. Have everyone chant them, write them and tell what spelling changes are needed: **marry**, **write**, **address**, **grab**, **swim**.

Lesson 25

Word Wall Words: broken frighten hidden went written
Suffix for Review: en

Give everyone a copy of the word wall (p. 149) and/or place the words on the classroom word wall.

Review:

Went is added to the word wall because it is a word that is often misspelled. The other words end with the suffix **en**. Have the root words and spelling changes identified and have each **en** word used in a sentence.

broken—broke with **e** dropped and **en** added. The chair was **broken**.

frighten—fright with **en** added. Do not **frighten** the baby.

hidden—hide with **e** dropped and **d** doubled. Where are the presents **hidden**?

written—write with **e** dropped and **t** doubled. I have **written** a poem.

Word Wall:

Call out the five words one at a time and have everyone chant the spelling three times for each word (for example: "f-r-i-g-h-t-e-n, frighten; f-r-i-g-h-t-e-n, frighten; f-r-i-g-h-t-e-n, frighten"). Next, have everyone write the five words as you give sentence clues.

1. That toy won't work because it is _____.
2. Last summer my whole family _____ to the beach.
3. I don't know where the presents are _____.
4. The loud noise will _____ the baby.
5. I have _____ five stories this year.

Lessons 26-30
Suffixes: y; al

Lesson 26

Letters: a e h h l t y
Words: eat ate let yet the they late hate health healthy

Make Words: Distribute the letters and have everyone write the capitals on the back. After each word is made, show the correct spelling. Make sure everyone has each word spelled correctly before doing the next word. Keep the lesson fast paced.

1. Take 3 letters and spell **eat**. <u>I **eat** cereal for breakfast.</u>
2. Move the letters around and spell **ate**. <u>Yesterday I **ate** Cheerios.®</u>
3. Take 3 letters and spell **let**. <u>I hope your mom will **let** you come over and play.</u>
4. Change 1 letter and spell **yet**. <u>Lunch is not ready **yet**.</u>
5. Take 3 letters and spell **the**. <u>**The** bus is coming.</u>
6. Add 1 letter and spell **they**. <u>**They** are all getting on the bus.</u>
7. Use 4 letters to spell **late**. <u>I hope we won't be **late** for school.</u>
8. Change 1 letter and spell **hate**. <u>I **hate** it when the bus is late.</u>
9. Use 6 letters to spell **health**. <u>The doctor said my **health** is very good.</u>
10. It's time for the secret word. (Wait 1 minute and then give clues.) <u>She is trying to eat **healthy** food.</u>

Sort: Display the words on cards in the order they were made and have each word read aloud. Have the related words sorted. Then, have the rhyming words sorted.

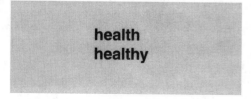

health
healthy

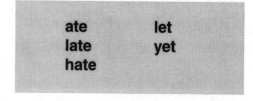

ate   let
late   yet
hate

Transfer: Say the following words and have everyone use the rhyming words to spell them:

skate   wet   date   mate

Word Wall: Have everyone look at the word wall. Call out the five new words (**broken, frighten, hidden, went, written**) and have everyone chant them and write them. Next to **written** and **hidden**, have them write the root words **write** and **hide**.

Lesson 27

Letters: a i n r y
Words: in an ran air any Ray Ira yarn rain rainy

Make Words: Distribute the letters and have everyone write the capitals on the back. After each word is made, show the correct spelling. Make sure everyone has each word spelled correctly before doing the next word. Keep the lesson fast paced.

1. Take 2 letters and spell **in**. <u>The gerbil is **in** its cage.</u>

2. Change 1 letter and spell **an**. <u>Can I please have **an** apple?</u>

3. Add 1 letter and spell **ran**. <u>We **ran** all the way to the park.</u>

4. Use 3 letters to spell **air**. <u>We need clean **air** to breathe.</u>

5. Use 3 letters to spell **any**. <u>I don't have **any** money.</u>

6. Use 3 letters to spell **Ray**. <u>**Ray** lives next door to me.</u>

7. Use 3 letters to spell **Ira**. <u>**Ira** is Ray's big brother.</u>

8. Use 4 letters to spell **yarn**. <u>You can knit a sweater with **yarn**.</u>

9. Use 4 letters to spell **rain**. <u>I hope it doesn't **rain** on Saturday.</u>

10. It's time for the secret word. (Wait 1 minute and then give clues.) <u>Friday was a **rainy** day.</u>

Sort: Display the words on cards in the order they were made and have each word read aloud. Have the related words sorted. Then, have the rhyming words sorted.

rain
rainy

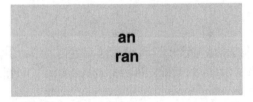

an
ran

Transfer: Say the following words and have everyone use the rhyming words to spell them:

man than clan plan

Word Wall: Have everyone look at the word wall and chant the spelling of the five new words (**went, written, broken, hidden, frighten**). Have everyone spell the following words using the word wall words as models: **tighten, spoken, bitten, brighten, woken.**

Lesson 28

Letters: a i u c l m s
Words: aim Sam slam clam calm sail mail claim music musical

Make Words: Distribute the letters and have everyone write the capitals on the back. After each word is made, show the correct spelling. Make sure everyone has each word spelled correctly before doing the next word. Keep the lesson fast paced.

1. Take 3 letters and spell **aim**. The hunter took **aim** at the deer.
2. Take 3 letters and spell **Sam**. **Sam** does not like green eggs and ham.
3. Add 1 letter and spell **slam**. Please don't **slam** the door.
4. Change 1 letter and spell **clam**. I like to eat **clam** chowder.
5. Move the letters around and spell **calm**. When the tornado struck, we tried to stay **calm**.
6. Use 4 letters again to spell **sail**. I like to watch the boats **sail** through the water.
7. Change 1 letter and spell **mail**. The **mail** comes around 1:00 in the afternoon.
8. Use 5 letters to spell **claim**. After the accident, we had to file a **claim** with the insurance company.
9. Use 5 letters again to spell **music**. What kind of **music** do you like?
10. It's time for the secret word. Add your letters to **music** and see what you get. (Wait 1 minute and then give clues.) We went to the theater to see the **musical**, *The Lion King.*

Sort: Display the words on cards in the order they were made and have each word read aloud. Have the related words sorted. Then, have the rhyming words sorted.

music
musical

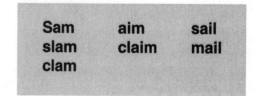

Sam	aim	sail
slam	claim	mail
clam		

Transfer: Say the following words and have everyone use the rhyming words to spell them:

jail tram ram fail

Word Wall: Call out five of the word wall words without their endings. Have everyone chant and write the following root words: **lunch, fright, broke, want, monkey**.

Lesson 29

Letters: a a i o l n n t
Words: an tan ant not into nail tail lion nation national

Make Words: Distribute the letters and have everyone write the capitals on the back. After each word is made, show the correct spelling. Make sure everyone has each word spelled correctly before doing the next word. Keep the lesson fast paced.

1. Take 2 letters and spell **an**. <u>**An** octopus has lots of legs.</u>
2. Add 1 letter and spell **tan**. <u>He came back from vacation with a nice **tan**.</u>
3. Move the letters around and spell **ant**. <u>An **ant** crawled across the table.</u>
4. Use 3 letters to spell **not**. <u>Making words is **not** hard work.</u>
5. Use 4 letters to spell **into**. <u>We had to climb **into** the cave.</u>
6. Use 4 letters again to spell **nail**. <u>I hammered the **nail** into the wall and hung the picture.</u>
7. Change 1 letter and spell **tail**. <u>The dog is wagging his **tail**.</u>
8. Use 4 letters again to spell **lion**. <u>The mother **lion** had 3 baby cubs.</u>
9. Use 6 letters to spell **nation**. <u>Our **nation** is united and strong.</u>
10. It's time for the secret word. Add your letters to **nation** and see what you have. (Wait 1 minute and then give clues.) <u>The Fourth of July is a **national** holiday.</u>

Sort: Display the words on cards in the order they were made and have each word read aloud. Have the related words sorted. Then, have the rhyming words sorted.

| nation | | an | nail |
| national | | tan | tail |

Transfer: Say the following words and have everyone use the rhyming words to spell them:

plan snail bran than

Word Wall: Call out five of the word wall words that need spelling changes without the endings. Have everyone chant them, write them and tell what spelling changes are needed: **write, hide, address, grab, swim.**

Lesson 30

Word Wall Words: healthy musical national rainy they
Suffixes for review: y; al

Give everyone a copy of the word wall (p. 150) and/or place the words on the classroom word wall.

Review:

They is added to the word wall because it is a word that is often misspelled. **Healthy** and **rainy** end with the suffix **y**. **Musical** and **national** end with the suffix **al**. Have the root words identified and have each root word and **y** or **al** word used in a sentence.

rainy—rain. A day that rains a lot is a **rainy** day.

healthy—health. If you have good health, you are **healthy**.

musical—music. Instruments you use to make music are called **musical** instruments.

national—nation. Holidays that the whole nation celebrates are **national** holidays.

Word Wall:

Call out the five words one at a time and have everyone chant the spelling three times for each word (for example: "r-a-i-n-y, rainy; r-a-i-n-y, rainy; r-a-i-n-y, rainy"). Next, have everyone write the five words as you give sentence clues.

1. The Fourth of July is a _____ holiday.

2. I am losing weight by exercising and eating _____ foods.

3. My friends have gone but _____ were here a few minutes ago.

4. We have to play inside on a _____ day.

5. Drums are my favorite _____ instrument.

Lesson 31

Letters: e i o g h m n s t
Words: sing song home some thin thing night might eight something

Make Words: Distribute the letters and have everyone write the capitals on the back. After each word is made, show the correct spelling. Make sure everyone has each word spelled correctly before doing the next word. Keep the lesson fast paced.

1. Take 4 letters and spell **sing**. <u>We **sing** songs in music class.</u>
2. Change 1 letter and spell **song**. <u>What is your favorite **song**?</u>
3. Use 4 letters again to spell **home**. <u>I stayed **home** yesterday because I was sick.</u>
4. Change 1 letter and spell **some**. <u>I ate **some** chicken soup for lunch.</u>
5. Use 4 letters again to spell **thin**. <u>She cut me a **thin** piece of cake.</u>
6. Add 1 letter and spell **thing**. <u>One **thing** I hate to do is to take out the trash.</u>
7. Move the letters around and spell **night**. <u>On Friday **night**, we go to the mall.</u>
8. Change 1 letter and spell **might**. <u>We **might** go to a movie this Friday.</u>
9. Change 1 letter and spell **eight**. <u>I invited **eight** people to my party.</u>
10. The secret word is a compound word made up of 2 words you already made. (Wait 1 minute and then give clues.) <u>We were trying to think of **something** to do.</u>

Sort: Display the words on cards in the order they were made and have each word read aloud. Have the related words sorted. Then, have the rhyming words sorted.

some
thing
something

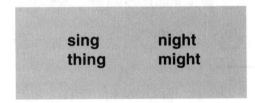

sing   night
thing   might

Transfer: Say the following words and have everyone use the rhyming words to spell them:

bring string tight slight

Word Wall: Have everyone look at the word wall. Call out the five new words and have everyone chant them and write them: **healthy**, **musical**, **national**, **rainy**, **they**.

Lesson 32

Letters: e e e o n r v y
Words: on Ron one very over oven even ever never every everyone

Make Words: Distribute the letters and have everyone write the capitals on the back. After each word is made, show the correct spelling. Make sure everyone has each word spelled correctly before doing the next word. Keep the lesson fast paced.

1. Take 2 letters and spell **on**. We rode **on** the bus.
2. Add 1 letter and spell **Ron**. My friend's name is **Ron**.
3. Use 3 letters to spell **one**. Our soccer team was number **one**!
4. Take 4 letters and spell **very**. Our coach was **very** happy with us.
5. Use 4 letters again to spell **over**. The game will be **over** around 7:00.
6. Change 1 letter and spell **oven**. The cookies are baking in the **oven**.
7. Change 1 letter and spell **even**. Two, four, and six are **even** numbers.
8. Change 1 letter and spell **ever**. Do you **ever** wish you could fly?
9. Add 1 letter and spell **never**. I have **never** flown on an airplane.
10. Use 5 letters again to spell **every**. I do my homework **every** night.
11. The secret word is a compound word made up of 2 words you already made. (Wait 1 minute and then give clues.) **Everyone** came to watch the game.

Sort: Display the words on cards in the order they were made and have each word read aloud. Have the related words sorted. Then, have the rhyming words sorted.

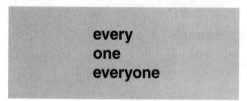

every
one
everyone

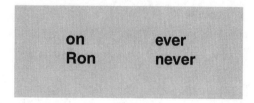

on   ever
Ron   never

Transfer: Say the following words and have everyone use the rhyming words to spell them:

con lever clever sever

Word Wall: Have everyone look at the word wall and chant the spelling of the five new words. Spell some words ("wealth, w-e-a-l-t-h") and have everyone decide if they will make a word with **y** or **al** added and write the new words: **wealthy**, **magical**, **logical**, **personal**, **sunny**.

Lesson 33

Letters: a o b d n y y
Words: an any and Dan Don nod band bond body anybody

Make Words: Distribute the letters and have everyone write the capitals on the back. After each word is made, show the correct spelling. Make sure everyone has each word spelled correctly before doing the next word. Keep the lesson fast paced.

1. Take 2 letters and spell **an**. We each had **an** ice cream cone.
2. Add 1 letter and spell **any**. I didn't eat **any** cake.
3. Change 1 letter and spell **and**. I have two cats **and** a dog.
4. Move the letters around and spell **Dan**. **Dan** is in the fourth grade.
5. Change 1 letter and spell **Don**. **Don** and Dan are best friends.
6. Move the letters around and spell **nod**. **Nod** your head if you agree.
7. Take 4 letters and spell **band**. The **band** marched in the parade.
8. Change 1 letter and spell **bond**. My grandma gave me a savings **bond** for my birthday.
9. Use 4 letters again to spell **body**. The Atlantic Ocean is a large **body** of water.
10. The secret word is a compound word made up of 2 words you already made. (Wait 1 minute and then give clues.) Can **anybody** figure out the secret word?

Sort: Display the words on cards in the order they were made and have each word read aloud. Have the related words sorted. Then, have the rhyming words sorted.

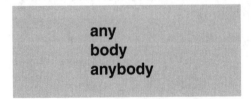

any
body
anybody

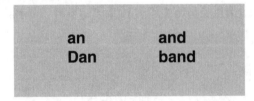

an	and
Dan	band

Transfer: Say the following words and have everyone use the rhyming words to spell them:

stand grand span plan

Word Wall: Call out five of the word wall words without their endings. Have everyone chant and write these root words: **music, health, nation, rain, fright.**

Lesson 34

Make Words: Distribute the letters and have everyone write the capitals on the back. After each word is made, show the correct spelling. Make sure everyone has each word spelled correctly before doing the next word. Keep the lesson fast paced.

1. Take 2 letters and spell **an**. We had **an** easy math test today.
2. Add 1 letter and spell **any**. I don't have **any** money.
3. Take 3 letters and spell **new**. I got a **new** box of crayons.
4. Use 3 letters and spell **hen**. The **hen** was in the barn.
5. Add 1 letter and spell **when**. **When** will you be home?
6. Use 4 letters to spell **year**. I was gone for a whole **year**.
7. Change 1 letter and spell **near**. Do you live **near** the school?
8. Use 4 letters again and spell **were**. Where **were** you?
9. Add 1 letter and spell **where**. I know **where** you were.
10. Take 5 letters and spell **newer**. My sister's bike is **newer** than mine is.
11. The secret word is a compound word made up of 2 words you already made. (Wait 1 minute and then give clues.) You can sit **anywhere** you would like.

Sort: Display the words on cards in the order they were made and have each word read aloud. Have the related words sorted. Then, have the rhyming words sorted.

any   new
where   newer
anywhere

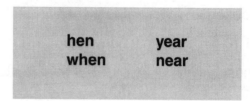

hen   year
when   near

Transfer: Say the following words and have everyone use the rhyming words to spell them:

clear fear then spear

Word Wall: Call out five of the commonly misspelled words. Have everyone chant them and write them: **are, our, what, went, they**.

Lesson 35

Give everyone a copy of the word wall (p. 151) and/or place the words on the classroom word wall.

Review:

Were is added to the word wall because it is a word that is often misspelled. The other four words are compound words. Have the words that make up each compound word identified and have the compound words used in a sentence.

anybody—any body. Is **anybody** home?

anywhere—any where. My cat goes **anywhere** she wants to.

everyone—every one. **Everyone** enjoyed the game.

something—some thing. I will get **something** nice for my friend's birthday.

Word Wall:

Call out the five words one at a time and have everyone chant the spelling three times for each word. Next, have everyone write the five words as you give sentence clues.

1. Let's think of _____ fun to do.

2. Has _____ seen my book?

3. I have looked and looked but I can't find that book _____.

4. I invited 10 people to my party and _____ came.

5. My friends _____ all here yesterday.

Lessons 36-40
Contractions

Lesson 36

Letters: e e h r t y '
Words: Ty try her the they tree here there three they're

Make Words: Distribute the letters and have everyone write the capitals on the back. **Point out the apostrophe, which will be needed to spell a contraction.** After each word is made, show the correct spelling. Make sure everyone has each word spelled correctly before doing the next word. Keep the lesson fast paced.

1. Take 2 letters and spell the name **Ty**. Ty Cobb was a famous baseball player.

2. Add 1 letter and spell **try**. I will **try** to come over to your house.

3. Use 3 letters to spell **her**. My sister has **her** own room.

4. Use 3 letters to spell **the**. **The** class is planning a surprise for **the** teacher.

5. Use 4 letters to spell **they**. My friends said **they** would pick me up at 7:00.

6. Use 4 letters again to spell **tree**. We have a big **tree** in our yard.

7. Use 4 letters again to spell **here**. Your notebook is right **here**.

8. Add 1 letter and spell **there**. **There** is a good movie on TV tonight.

9. Move the letters around and spell **three**. I have **three** cousins.

10. Use the apostrophe and all your letters to spell a contraction that is the secret word. (Wait 1 minute, then give a clue. The contraction means "they are.") My friends said **they're** coming over to my house later.

Sort: Display the words on cards in the order they were made and have each word read aloud. Have the related words sorted. Then, have the rhyming words sorted.

they		tree	try
they're		three	Ty

Transfer: Say the following words and have everyone use the rhyming words to spell them:

free fry flee fly

Word Wall: Have everyone look at the word wall. Call out the five new words and have everyone chant them and write them: **everyone, anybody, anywhere, were, something.**

Lesson 37

Make Words: Distribute the letters and have everyone write the capitals on the back. **Today's lesson also has an apostrophe.** After each word is made, show the correct spelling. Make sure everyone has each word spelled correctly before doing the next word. Keep the lesson fast paced.

1. Use 2 letters to spell **do**. It is time to **do** your homework.

2. Take 3 letters and spell **not**. The homework is **not** hard.

3. Change 1 letter and spell **dot**. All Internet addresses have a **dot** in them.

4. Use 3 letters to spell **one**. One day the bus broke down and we were late to school.

5. Add 1 letter and spell **done**. What have you **done** to get better at spelling?

6. Use 4 letters again to spell **sent**. I **sent** a birthday card to my aunt.

7. Change 1 letter and spell **dent**. The car has a **dent** in the back door.

8. Change 1 letter and add your apostrophe to spell **don't**. **Don't** tell me what to do.

9. Use 4 letters again to spell **does**. **Does** your brother go to school?

10. Use the apostrophe and all your letters to spell a contraction that is the secret word. (Wait 1 minute, then give a clue. The contraction means "does not.") My teacher **doesn't** like it when we get noisy.

Sort: Display the words on cards in the order they were made and have each word read aloud. Have the related words sorted. Then, have the rhyming words sorted.

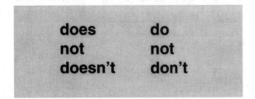

does	do
not	not
doesn't	don't

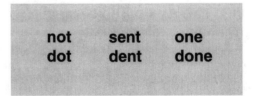

not	sent	one
dot	dent	done

Transfer: Say the following words and have everyone use the rhyming words to spell them:

none spot bent spent

Word Wall: Have everyone look at the word wall and chant the spelling of the five new words (**were, anybody, anywhere, something, everyone**). Call out other compound words that combine the words and have everyone write the following words: **someone, somewhere, everything, anything, everybody**.

Lesson 38

Letters: o u d l n t w '
Words: do old told undo down town won't don't donut would wouldn't

Make Words: Distribute the letters (and the apostrophe) and have everyone write the capitals on the back. After each word is made, show the correct spelling. Make sure everyone has each word spelled correctly before doing the next word. Keep the lesson fast paced.

1. Take 2 letters and spell **do**. <u>What sport **do** you like best?</u>

2. Take 3 letters and spell **old**. <u>How **old** are you?</u>

3. Add 1 letter and spell **told**. <u>My friend **told** me a secret.</u>

4. Use 4 letters again to spell **undo**. <u>It is easier to do something than it is to **undo** it.</u>

5. Use 4 letters again to spell **down**. <u>We rode our bikes fast **down** the hill.</u>

6. Change 1 letter and spell **town**. <u>The post office and the library are in the center of **town**.</u>

7. Use 4 letters and the apostrophe to spell **won't**. <u>I **won't** tell the secret.</u>

8. Change 1 letter and spell the contraction **don't**. <u>**Don't** worry about me.</u>

9. Remove the apostrophe and add 1 letter and spell **donut**. <u>I ate a jelly **donut**.</u>

10. Use 5 letters again to spell **would**. <u>I **would** like to go to Hawaii.</u>

11. Use the apostrophe and all your letters to spell a contraction that is the secret word. (Wait 1 minute, then give a clue. The contraction means "would not.") <u>I wanted to go but my mom **wouldn't** let me.</u>

Sort: Display the words on cards in the order they were made and have each word read aloud. Have the related words sorted. Then, have the rhyming words sorted.

would	do		old	down	won't
wouldn't	undo		told	town	don't

Transfer: Say the following words and have everyone use the rhyming words to spell them:

brown crown clown scold

Word Wall: Call out five of the word wall words that double the consonant before endings are added. Have everyone chant them, write them and tell what spelling changes are needed: **swimming, stopping, grabbed, hidden, written**.

Lesson 39

Make Words: Distribute the letters (and the apostrophe) and have everyone write the capitals on the back. After each word is made, show the correct spelling. Make sure everyone has each word spelled correctly before doing the next word. Keep the lesson fast paced.

1. Take 2 letters and spell **do**. What **do** you like to **do** after school?

2. Take 3 letters and spell **not**. I do **not** like rainy days.

3. Use 4 letters to spell **shot**. The doctor gave me a **shot** to get rid of the infection.

4. Use 4 letters again to spell **sold**. I **sold** my old bike and am saving for a new one.

5. Use 4 letters and the apostrophe to spell **don't**. **Don't** tell the secret.

6. Add 1 letter and remove the apostrophe to spell **donut**. I ate a chocolate **donut**.

7. Use 5 letters again to spell **sound**. It was so quiet I couldn't hear a **sound**.

8. Change 1 letter and spell **hound**. My uncle's hunting dog is a **hound**.

9. Use 6 letters to spell **unsold**. We gave all the **unsold** items from the yard sale to charity.

10. Use 6 letters to spell **should**. You **should** be able to figure out the secret word.

11. Use the apostrophe and all your letters to spell a contraction that is the secret word. (Wait 1 minute, then give a clue. The contraction means "should not.") My mom says I **shouldn't** tease my little sister.

Sort: Display the words on cards in the order they were made and have each word read aloud. Have the related words sorted. Then, have the rhyming words sorted.

should	sold	not	sound
shouldn't	unsold	shot	hound

Transfer: Say the following words and have everyone use the rhyming words to spell them:

round ground slot plot

Word Wall: Call out five words that can be spelled by using the compound word they are part of. Have everyone chant them and write them: **some**, **every**, **any**, **where**, **one**.

Lesson 40

Word Wall Words: don't doesn't shouldn't they're wouldn't
Review: Compounds

Give everyone a copy of the word wall (p. 152) and/or place the words on the classroom word wall.

Review:

All five new words are contractions. Have the two words that make up the contraction identified and have each contraction used in a sentence.

don't—do not. <u>I **don't** like peas.</u>

doesn't—does not. <u>My brother **doesn't** like broccoli.</u>

shouldn't—should not. <u>My mom says I **shouldn't** talk to strangers.</u>

they're—they are. <u>My friends said **they're** coming over at 7:00.</u>

wouldn't—would not. <u>My mom said she **wouldn't** be late.</u>

Word Wall:

Call out the five words one at a time and have everyone chant the spelling three times for each word. Have everyone make a "clicking sound" and draw the apostrophe in the air to show where the apostrophe is. Next, have everyone write the five words as you give these clues.

1. This contraction means "they are."

2. This contraction means "would not."

3. This contraction means "does not."

4. This contraction means "should not."

5. This contraction means "do not."

Lessons 41-45
Suffixes: er; est

Lesson 41

Letters: a e d h r s t
Words: had hard date hate heat heart earth shade trade hardest

Make Words: Distribute the letters and have everyone write the capitals on the back. After each word is made, show the correct spelling. Make sure everyone has each word spelled correctly before doing the next word. Keep the lesson fast paced.

1. Take 3 letters and spell **had**. My brother **had** his tonsils removed.
2. Add 1 letter and spell **hard**. That was a **hard** test.
3. Use 4 letters to spell **date**. The **date** of our party is February 14.
4. Change 1 letter and spell **hate**. I love spinach but I **hate** turnips.
5. Move the letters around and spell **heat**. Please turn up the **heat**.
6. Add 1 letter and spell **heart**. Your **heart** pumps blood through your body.
7. Move the letters around and spell **earth**. **Earth** is the planet that we live on.
8. Use 5 letters to spell **shade**. Let's sit in the **shade** and eat our lunch.
9. Change the first 2 letters and spell **trade**. I'll **trade** you half my apple for a cookie.
10. It's time for the secret word. Add your letters to one of the words we already made and you will have it. (Give clues after 1 minute.) Math is the **hardest** subject for me.

Sort: Display the words on cards in the order they were made and have each word read aloud. Have the related words sorted. Then, have the rhyming words sorted.

hard **hardest**	**date** **trade** **hate** **shade**

Transfer: Say the following words and have everyone use the rhyming words to spell them:

late spade wade plate

Word Wall: Call out the five contractions. Have everyone chant them and write them: **don't**, **doesn't**, **wouldn't**, **shouldn't**, **they're**.

Lesson 42

Letters: a e e i s s t
Words: at ate eat sit sat set seat east eats easiest

Make Words: Distribute the letters and have everyone write the capitals on the back. After each word is made, show the correct spelling. Make sure everyone has each word spelled correctly before doing the next word. Keep the lesson fast paced.

1. Take 2 letters and spell **at**. <u>Pick me up **at** the mall.</u>

2. Add 1 letter and spell **ate**. <u>We **ate** pizza at the party.</u>

3. Move the letters around and spell **eat**. <u>My dog will **eat** anything.</u>

4. Use 3 letters to spell **sit**. <u>Let's **sit** in the front row.</u>

5. Change 1 letter and spell **sat**. <u>I **sat** next to my friend.</u>

6. Change 1 letter and spell **set**. <u>Please **set** the table.</u>

7. Add 1 letter and spell **seat**. <u>I got the last **seat** on the bus.</u>

8. Move the letters around and spell **east**. <u>The sun rises in the **east** and sets in the west.</u>

9. Move the letters around and spell **eats**. <u>My cat **eats** cat food.</u>

10. It's time for the secret word. (Wait 1 minute and then give clues.) <u>Math is my brother's hardest subject but it's my **easiest** one.</u>

Sort: Display the words on cards in the order they were made and have each word read aloud. Have the related words sorted. Then, have the rhyming words sorted.

eat
eats

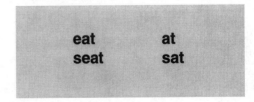

eat	at
seat	sat

Transfer: Say the following words and have everyone use the rhyming words to spell them:

beat heat cheat chat

Word Wall: Call out the words the contractions stand for ("they are," "do not," "would not," "should not," "does not"). Have everyone chant the spelling of the contractions and write them: **they're, don't, wouldn't, shouldn't, doesn't.**

Lesson 43

Letters: a e f r s t
Words: ear fear tear fast east feast tears stare after faster

Make Words: Distribute the letters and have everyone write the capitals on the back. After each word is made, show the correct spelling. Make sure everyone has each word spelled correctly before doing the next word. Keep the lesson fast paced.

1. Take 3 letters and spell **ear**. My dog has one white **ear** and one black **ear**.

2. Add 1 letter and spell **fear**. Some people have a terrible **fear** of snakes.

3. Add 1 letter and spell **tear**. She started to cry and one **tear** rolled down her cheek.

4. Use 4 letters to spell **fast**. He is a very **fast** runner.

5. Change 1 letter and spell **east**. We drove **east** to the Atlantic Ocean.

6. Add 1 letter and spell **feast**. We had a Thanksgiving **feast**.

7. Use 5 letters and spell **tears**. When my dog died, I cried buckets of **tears**.

8. Move the letters around and spell **stare**. It is not polite to **stare** at people.

9. Use 5 letters to spell **after**. We went to the park **after** school.

10. It's time for the secret word. Add your letters to a word we already made. (After 1 minute, give clues.) I can run **faster** than most of my friends.

Sort: Display the words on cards in the order they were made and have each word read aloud. Have the related words sorted. Then, have the rhyming words sorted.

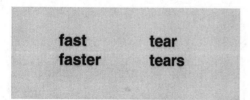

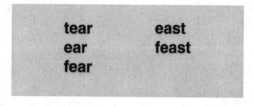

Transfer: Say the following words and have everyone use the rhyming words to spell them:

beast yeast year clear

Word Wall: Call out five compound words including the four on the wall and one that can be spelled by combining words. Have everyone chant them and write them: **anybody, anywhere, something, everyone, everything**.

Lesson 44

Letters: a e e i h r v
Words: are air ear hear hair have hive hire ever heavier

Make Words: Distribute the letters and have everyone write the capitals on the back. After each word is made, show the correct spelling. Make sure everyone has each word spelled correctly before doing the next word. Keep the lesson fast paced.

1. Take 3 letters and spell **are**. There **are** five people in my family.

2. Take 3 letters and spell **air**. Open the windows and let in some fresh **air**.

3. Change 1 letter and spell **ear**. My dog scratches her **ear**.

4. Add 1 letter and spell **hear**. My grandfather doesn't **hear** very well.

5. Change 1 letter and spell **hair**. The girl has long red **hair**.

6. Take 4 letters and spell **have**. Do you **have** a red crayon?

7. Change 1 letter and spell **hive**. Bees live in a **hive**.

8. Change 1 letter and spell **hire**. When I am 16, my dad is going to **hire** me to work in the store.

9. Use 4 letters again to spell **ever**. Did you **ever** stay up all night?

10. It's time for the secret word. (Wait 1 minute and then give clues.) The box I am carrying is **heavier** than the one you are carrying.

Sort: Display the words on cards in the order they were made and have each word read aloud. Have the rhyming words sorted.

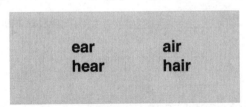

| ear | air |
| hear | hair |

Transfer: Say the following words and have everyone use the rhyming words to spell them:

chair stair spear shear

Word Wall: Call out five contractions including three that are on the word wall and two that can be spelled by using the contractions there as models. Have everyone chant the spelling of the contractions and write them: **wouldn't, shouldn't, couldn't, don't, won't.** Point out that **couldn't** stands for "could not" and **won't** stands for "will not."

Lesson 45

Word Wall Words: easiest faster hardest have heavier
Suffixes for Review: er, est

Give everyone a copy of the word wall (p. 153) and/or place the words on the classroom word wall.

Review:

Have is added to the word wall because it is a word that is often misspelled. **Faster** and **heavier** end with the suffix **er**. The **er** suffix often adds the meaning of "more" to a word. **Hardest** and **easiest** end with **est**, which often adds the meaning of "most." Have the root words and spelling changes identified and have each **er** or **est** word used in a sentence.

faster—fast. My brother can run **faster** than I can.

heavier—heavy, **y** changes to **i**. Which package is **heavier**?

hardest—hard. This was the **hardest** test I have ever taken.

easiest—easy, **y** changes to **i**. My sister said her test was the **easiest**.

Word Wall:

Call out the five words one at a time and have everyone chant the spelling three times for each word. Next, have everyone write the five words as you give sentence clues.

1. The box I carried was much _____ than the one you carried.

2. The passenger train goes much _____ than the freight train.

3. The opposite of easiest is _____.

4. The opposite of hardest is _____.

5. Do you _____ an extra pencil I can borrow?

Lesson 46

Letters: a e l l m s s t
Words: all mall tall tell meal seal steal smell small smallest

Make Words: Distribute the letters and have everyone write the capitals on the back. After each word is made, show the correct spelling. Make sure everyone has each word spelled correctly before doing the next word. Keep the lesson fast paced.

1. Use 3 letters to spell **all**. We ate **all** the popcorn.

2. Add 1 letter and spell **mall**. They are building a big new shopping **mall**.

3. Change 1 letter and spell **tall**. The opposite of short is **tall**.

4. Change 1 letter and spell **tell**. Do not **tell** anyone the secret.

5. Use 4 letters to spell **meal**. I went to McDonald's® and got a kid's **meal**.

6. Change 1 letter and spell **seal**. The **seal** did tricks with a ball.

7. Add 1 letter and spell **steal**. It is wrong to **steal** things.

8. Use 5 letters to spell **smell**. I walked in the door and could **smell** the cookies baking.

9. Change 1 letter and spell **small**. These jeans are too **small**.

10. It's time for the secret word. Add your letters to **small** and see what word you can make. (Wait 1 minute and then give clues.) I picked out my kitten and I chose the **smallest** one.

Sort: Display the words on cards in the order they were made and have each word read aloud. Have the related words sorted. Then, have the rhyming words sorted.

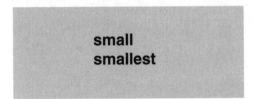

small		
smallest		

all	tell	meal
tall	smell	seal
mall		steal
small		

Transfer: Say the following words and have everyone use the rhyming words to spell them:

spell wall well real

Word Wall: Have everyone look at the word wall and chant and write the five new words: **have, faster, heavier, hardest, easiest.**

Lesson 47

Letter: e i b g g s t
Words: big beg bet get set sit bit bite best biggest

Make Words: Distribute the letters and have everyone write the capitals on the back. After each word is made, show the correct spelling. Make sure everyone has each word spelled correctly before doing the next word. Keep the lesson fast paced.

1. Take 3 letters and spell **big**. I want the **big** candy bar.
2. Change 1 letter and spell **beg**. My dog will sit and **beg** for food.
3. Change 1 letter and spell **bet**. I **bet** you can't hold your breath until I count to 20!
4. Change 1 letter and spell **get**. It is time for us to **get** going.
5. Change 1 letter and spell **set**. We bought a new **set** of dishes.
6. Change 1 letter and spell **sit**. Please **sit** down!
7. Change 1 letter and spell **bit**. The dog **bit** the boy.
8. Add 1 letter and spell **bite**. Most dogs do not **bite** people.
9. Use 4 letters to spell **best**. What is the **best** book you ever read?
10. It's time for the secret word. Add your letters to a word we already made to figure it out. (Wait 1 minute and then give clues.) I opened the **biggest** present last.

Sort: Display the words on cards in the order they were made and have each word read aloud. Have the related words sorted. Then, have the rhyming words sorted.

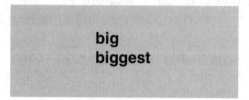

big
biggest

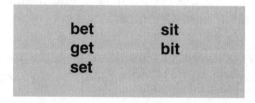

bet   sit
get   bit
set

Transfer: Say the following words and have everyone use the rhyming words to spell them:

let lit jet vet

Word Wall: Call out five of the root words that can be spelled from word wall words. Have everyone chant them, write them and tell what spelling changes are needed: **heavy, easy, write, fry, marry.**

Lesson 48

Letters: e i h n n r t
Words: in tin ten hen then thin tire hire their thinner

Make Words: Distribute the letters and have everyone write the capitals on the back. After each word is made, show the correct spelling. Make sure everyone has each word spelled correctly before doing the next word. Keep the lesson fast paced.

1. Take 2 letters and spell **in**. <u>We swim **in** the pool.</u>

2. Add 1 letter and spell **tin**. <u>We recycle **tin** cans.</u>

3. Change 1 letter and spell **ten**. <u>Five plus five equals **ten**.</u>

4. Change 1 letter and spell **hen**. <u>The **hen** was sitting on her eggs.</u>

5. Add 1 letter and spell **then**. <u>We walked home and **then** we fixed a snack.</u>

6. Change 1 letter and spell **thin**. <u>The opposite of thick is **thin**.</u>

7. Use 4 letters to spell **tire**. <u>I need a new **tire** for my bike.</u>

8. Change 1 letter and spell **hire**. <u>The new factory will **hire** a lot of people.</u>

9. Use 5 letters to spell **their**. <u>The twins had **their** birthday party at **their** house.</u>

10. It's time for the secret word. Add your letters to a word we already made and you can figure it out. (Wait 1 minute and then give clues.) <u>My mom went on a diet and is a lot **thinner** than she used to be.</u>

Sort: Display the words on cards in the order they were made and have each word read aloud. Have the related words sorted. Then, have the rhyming words sorted.

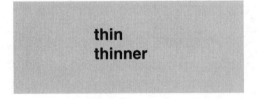

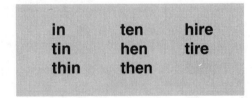

Transfer: Say the following words and have everyone use the rhyming words to spell them:

when   fire   spin   wire

Word Wall: Call out five of the root words that can be spelled from word wall words. Have everyone chant and write these root words: **hard, fast, nation, music, health.**

Lesson 49

Letters: i e u f n n r

Words: if in fin fun run ruin nine fine fire funnier

Make Words: Distribute the letters and have everyone write the capitals on the back. After each word is made, show the correct spelling. Make sure everyone has each word spelled correctly before doing the next word. Keep the lesson fast paced.

1. Take 2 letters and spell **if**. You can go **if** you finish your work.
2. Change 1 letter and spell **in**. What month were you born **in**?
3. Add 1 letter and spell **fin**. When the porpoise jumped out of the water, I saw his **fin**.
4. Change 1 letter and spell **fun**. We had **fun** at the zoo.
5. Change 1 letter and spell **run**. When it started raining, we started to **run**.
6. Add 1 letter and spell **ruin**. If it rains, it will **ruin** our plans for a picnic.
7. Use 4 letters again to spell **nine**. A baseball team has **nine** players.
8. Change 1 letter and spell **fine**. I hope everyone is feeling **fine** today.
9. Change 1 letter and spell **fire**. Let's build a **fire** in the fireplace.
10. It's time for the secret word. (Wait 1 minute and then give clues.) That cartoon was **funnier** than the one we watched last week.

Sort: Display the words on cards in the order they were made and have each word read aloud. Have the rhyming words sorted.

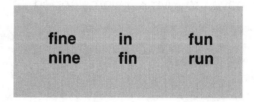

fine	in	fun
nine	fin	run

Transfer: Say the following words and have everyone use the rhyming words to spell them:

shine   spine   spin   spun

Word Wall: Call out five of the commonly misspelled words. Have everyone chant and write these root words: **were**, **have**, **are**, **our**, **what**.

Lesson 50

Word Wall Words: biggest funnier smallest their thinner
Suffixes for Review: er; est

Give everyone a copy of the word wall (p. 154) and/or place the words on the classroom word wall.

Review:

Their is added to the word wall because it is a word that is often confused with **there** or the contraction **they're**. **Their** is the word that we use when we refer to people. **Funnier** and **thinner** end with the suffix **er**. **Biggest** and **smallest** end with **est**. Have the root words and spelling changes identified and have each **er** or **est** word used in a sentence.

funnier—funny, **y** changes to **i**. That show was **funnier** than the last one.

thinner—thin, **n** is doubled. Cut the cake into **thinner** slices.

biggest—big, **g** is doubled. I wanted the **biggest** piece.

smallest—small. He gave me the **smallest** piece.

Word Wall:

Call out the five words one at a time and have everyone chant the spelling three times for each word. Next, have everyone write the five words as you give sentence clues.

1. Everyone thought our comedy skit was _____ than the other one.

2. The opposite of thicker is _____.

3. The opposite of biggest is _____.

4. The opposite of smallest is _____.

5. Everyone brought _____ pets to the pet show.

Lesson 51

Letters: a e e c h r t
Words: eat heat each here there reach teach cheat cheater teacher

Make Words: Distribute the letters and have everyone write the capitals on the back. After each word is made, show the correct spelling. Make sure everyone has each word spelled correctly before doing the next word. Keep the lesson fast paced.

1. Take 3 letters and spell **eat**. We **eat** lunch at 12:30.

2. Add 1 letter and spell **heat**. The **heat** is set on 72 degrees.

3. Use 4 letters again to spell **each**. My mom gave us **each** a dollar to spend.

4. Use 4 letters again to spell **here**. Wait **here** until I come back.

5. Add 1 letter and spell **there**. My friends are over **there**.

6. Use 5 letters again to spell **reach**. Can you **reach** the top shelf?

7. Change 1 letter and spell **teach**. I will **teach** you how to play the game.

8. Move the letters around and spell **cheat**. I won't play with people who **cheat**.

9. It's time for the secret word. These letters make 2 secret words. Add your letters to 2 of the words we made and see it you can figure them out. (Wait 1 minute and then give clues.) My **teacher** does not want anyone to be a **cheater**.

Sort: Display the words on cards in the order they were made and have each word read aloud. Have the related words sorted. Then, have the rhyming words sorted.

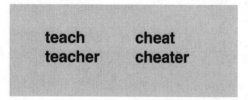

teach   cheat
teacher   cheater

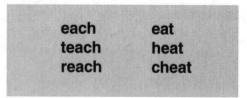

each   eat
teach   heat
reach   cheat

Transfer: Say the following words and have everyone use the rhyming words to spell them:

peach   preach   wheat   treat

Word Wall: Have everyone look at the word wall and chant and write the five new words: **their, thinner, funnier, smallest, biggest**.

Lesson 52

Letters: e o u c m p r s t
Words: come some sore more core score store sport customer computers

Make Words: Distribute the letters and have everyone write the capitals on the back. After each word is made, show the correct spelling. Make sure everyone has each word spelled correctly before doing the next word. Keep the lesson fast paced.

1. Use 4 letters to spell **come**. Please **come** over and play with me.
2. Change 1 letter and spell **some**. Do you want **some** cookies?
3. Change 1 letter and spell **sore**. I have a **sore** throat.
4. Change 1 letter and spell **more**. Is there any **more** cake?
5. Change 1 letter and spell **core**. You don't eat the apple **core**.
6. Add 1 letter and spell **score**. The **score** was 3 to 1 and our team was winning.
7. Change 1 letter and spell **store**. Let's walk down to the **store**.
8. Use 5 letters to spell **sport**. Basketball is my favorite **sport**.
9. Use 8 letters to spell **customer**. The **customer** bought five books.
10. It's time for the secret word. (Wait 1 minute and then give clues.) I like playing games on **computers**.

Sort: Display the words on cards in the order they were made and have each word read aloud. Have the rhyming words sorted.

come	sore
some	more
	core
	score
	store

Transfer: Say the following words and have everyone use the rhyming words to spell them:

shore tore wore chore

Word Wall: Call out five words that end in **est** that can be spelled using word wall words as models. Have everyone chant them, write them and tell what spelling changes are needed: **fastest, heaviest, thinnest, funniest, healthiest.**

Lesson 53

Letters: a e k r s t
Words: eat ate Kate rate rake take seat east skate skater

Make Words: Distribute the letters and have everyone write the capitals on the back. After each word is made, show the correct spelling. Make sure everyone has each word spelled correctly before doing the next word. Keep the lesson fast paced.

1. Take 3 letters and spell **eat**. What time do we **eat**?

2. Move the letters around and spell **ate**. We **ate** at the Pizza Hut®.

3. Add 1 letter and spell **Kate**. The baby's name is **Kate**.

4. Change 1 letter and spell **rate**. How would you **rate** that movie?

5. Change 1 letter and spell **rake**. I like to **rake** leaves.

6. Change 1 letter and spell **take**. Please **take** these cookies to Grandma's.

7. Use 4 letters to spell **seat**. Our **seat** was in the front row of the bus.

8. Move the letters around and spell **east**. Georgia is **east** of Texas.

9. Use 5 letters to spell **skate**. I like to ice **skate**.

10. It's time for the secret word. (Wait 1 minute and then give clues.) The best **skater** won the championship.

Sort: Display the words on cards in the order they were made and have each word read aloud. Have the related words sorted. Then, have the rhyming words sorted.

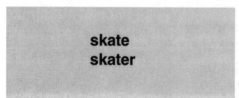

skate	ate	eat	rake
skater	Kate	seat	take
	skate		
	rate		

Transfer: Say the following words and have everyone use the rhyming words to spell them:

> treat brake snake state

Word Wall: Call out five words that end in **er** that can be spelled using word wall words as models. Have everyone chant them, write them and tell what spelling changes are needed: **harder**, **easier**, **bigger**, **smaller**, **rainier**.

Lesson 54

Letters: e i n n r s w
Words: is in win new news wire rise wise wiser winners

Make Words: Distribute the letters and have everyone write the capitals on the back. After each word is made, show the correct spelling. Make sure everyone has each word spelled correctly before doing the next word. Keep the lesson fast paced.

1. Take 2 letters and spell **is**. <u>The woman **is** shopping.</u>
2. Change 1 letter and spell **in**. <u>He ran **in** the marathon.</u>
3. Add 1 letter and spell **win**. <u>He did not **win** the race.</u>
4. Use 3 letters to spell **new**. <u>I have a **new** bike.</u>
5. Add 1 letter and spell **news**. <u>We watch the **news** on CNN every night.</u>
6. Use 4 letters to spell **wire**. <u>They are going to **wire** our classroom so we can get on the Internet.</u>
7. Use 4 letters again to spell **rise**. <u>It rained for three days and the water in the lake began to **rise**.</u>
8. Change 1 letter and spell **wise**. <u>I wonder why they say an owl is **wise**.</u>
9. Add 1 letter and spell **wiser**. <u>As we get older, we get **wiser**.</u>
10. It's time for the secret word. Add your letters to a word we already made and you will have the secret word. (Wait 1 minute and then give clues.) <u>The **winners** of the raffle won gift certificates to a toy store.</u>

Sort: Display the words on cards in the order they were made and have each word read aloud. Have the related words sorted. Then, have the rhyming words sorted.

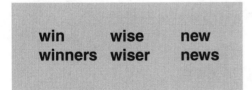

win   wise   new
winners   wiser   news

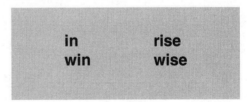

in   rise
win   wise

Transfer: Say the following words and have everyone use the rhyming words to spell them:

chin thin spin grin

Word Wall: Call out five root words that can be spelled from word wall words. Discuss spelling changes. Have everyone chant and write these root words: **small**, **big**, **thin**, **funny**, **heavy**.

Lesson 55

Word Wall Words: computers skater teacher there winners
Suffixes for Review: er; ers

Give everyone a copy of the word wall (p. 155) and/or place the words on the classroom word wall.

Review:

There is added to the word wall because it is a word that is often confused with **their** or the contraction, **they're. There** is the word that is the opposite of **here.** Underline the letters **h-e-r-e** in **there** as a clue to remembering how **there** is used. The other words all have the suffix **er.** Sometimes the suffix **er** indicates a person or thing that does something. Have the root words and spelling changes identified and explain the root word/**er** relationship.

computers—compute, **e** is dropped when **ers** is added. <u>**Computers** are machines that help us to compute or figure out things.</u>

teacher—teach. <u>The person who teaches is called a **teacher**.</u>

skater—skate, **e** is dropped when **er** is added. <u>A person who skates is a **skater**.</u>

winners—win, **n** is doubled. <u>The **winners** are the people who win.</u>

Word Wall:

Call out the five words one at a time and have everyone chant the spelling three times for each word. Next, have everyone write the five words as you give sentence clues.

1. My sister is a wonderful ice _____.

2. We can use _____ to play games or get information.

3. Every game has _____ and losers.

4. Our music _____ has a beautiful voice.

5. Your seat is over _____ by the window.

Lessons 56-60
Suffix: or

Lesson 56

Letters: e i o d r t
Words: Ed Ted die tie tied edit diet dirt tired tried editor

Make Words: Distribute the letters and have everyone write the capitals on the back. After each word is made, show the correct spelling. Make sure everyone has each word spelled correctly before doing the next word. Keep the lesson fast paced.

1. Take 2 letters and spell **Ed**. My favorite uncle is Uncle **Ed**.

2. Add 1 letter and spell **Ted**. Uncle **Ted** is my second favorite uncle.

3. Take 3 letters and spell **die**. My mom told me that our old dog might **die** soon.

4. Change 1 letter and spell **tie**. **Tie** your shoelaces.

5. Add 1 letter and spell **tied**. I **tied** them but they came untied.

6. Move the letters around and spell **edit**. Before we publish a piece of writing, we **edit** it.

7. Move the letters again and spell **diet**. My mom is on a **diet**.

8. Change 1 letter and spell **dirt**. After the game, I had **dirt** all over my uniform.

9. Use 5 letters to spell **tired**. We were all very **tired**.

10. Move the letters around and spell **tried**. I **tried** to call you, but you weren't home.

11. It's time for the secret word. Add your letters to a word we already made. (Wait 1 minute and then give clues.) The person who edits your writing is your **editor**.

Sort: Display the words on cards in the order they were made and have each word read aloud. Have the related words sorted. Then, have the rhyming words sorted.

edit	tie		die	Ed
editor	tied		tie	Ted

Transfer: Say the following words and have everyone use the rhyming words to spell them:

lie pie sled fled

Word Wall: Have everyone look at the word wall and chant and write the five new words: **there, computers, winners, teacher, skater**.

Lesson 57

Letters: a i o l r s
Words: is as air oil soil sail rail also solar sailor

Make Words: Distribute the letters and have everyone write the capitals on the back. After each word is made, show the correct spelling. Make sure everyone has each word spelled correctly before doing the next word. Keep the lesson fast paced.

1. Take 2 letters and spell **is**. Where **is** the game being played?
2. Change 1 letter and spell **as**. My sister is almost **as** tall **as** I am.
3. Use 3 letters to spell **air**. We need clean **air** to breathe.
4. Use 3 letters to spell **oil**. They drill deep into the ground to find **oil**.
5. Add 1 letter and spell **soil**. Plants need water, sun, and **soil** to grow.
6. Change 1 letter and spell **sail**. The boats **sail** into the harbor.
7. Change 1 letter and spell **rail**. Hold on to the **rail** when you go down the stairs.
8. Use 4 letters again to spell **also**. I like pizza and I **also** like spaghetti.
9. Use 5 letters to spell **solar**. We are learning about the **solar** system.
10. It's time for the secret word. Add your letters to a word we already made and figure it out. (Wait 1 minute and then give clues.) He joined the Navy and became a **sailor**.

Sort: Display the words on cards in the order they were made and have each word read aloud. Have the related words sorted. Then, have the rhyming words sorted.

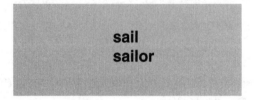

sail
sailor

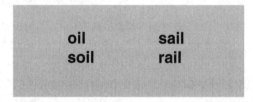

oil   sail
soil   rail

Transfer: Say the following words and have everyone use the rhyming words to spell them:

fail snail spoil coil

Word Wall: Call out the following five root words that can be spelled by dropping suffixes from word wall words. Spelling changes may be needed: **compute**, **teach**, **win**, **skate**, **funny**.

Make Words: Distribute the letters and have everyone write the capitals on the back. After each word is made, show the correct spelling. Make sure everyone has each word spelled correctly before doing the next word. Keep the lesson fast paced.

1. Take 2 letters and spell **go**. Where did you **go** on vacation?

2. Add 2 letters and spell **goes**. My family **goes** to the beach every summer.

3. Take 4 letters and spell **gone**. We have **gone** to the same beach for six years.

4. Use 4 letters again to spell **soon**. School will start **soon**.

5. Use 4 letters again to spell **nose**. One year, my **nose** got sunburned.

6. Change 1 letter and spell **rose**. I picked a **rose** for my teacher.

7. Move the letters around and spell **sore**. I cut my finger and it was very **sore**.

8. Add 1 letter and spell **snore**. Does your grandpa **snore** when he sleeps?

9. Use 6 letters and spell **sooner**. I wish we could get there **sooner**.

10. Use 6 letters again and spell **govern**. The president's job is to **govern** the country.

11. It's time for the secret word. Add your letters to **govern** and see what word you can make. (Wait 1 minute and then give clues.) The **governors** of all the states met in Washington.

Sort: Display the words on cards in the order they were made and have each word read aloud. Have the related words sorted. Then, have the rhyming words sorted.

govern	soon	go
governors	sooner	goes
		gone

nose	sore
rose	snore

Transfer: Say the following words and have everyone use the rhyming words to spell them:

bore store close hose

Word Wall: Call out five words that can be spelled by combining root words with other suffixes. Spelling changes may be needed: **teaching, teaches, skating, skated, computed.**

Lesson 59

Letters: a e e o l r t v
Words: at rat ate late over ever vote voter later travel elevator

Make Words: Distribute the letters and have everyone write the capitals on the back. After each word is made, show the correct spelling. Make sure everyone has each word spelled correctly before doing the next word. Keep the lesson fast paced.

1. Take 2 letters and spell **at**. <u>The game is **at** the high school.</u>
2. Add 1 letter and spell **rat**. <u>A **rat** is bigger than a mouse.</u>
3. Take 3 letters and spell **ate**. <u>We **ate** hot dogs at the ball game.</u>
4. Add 1 letter and spell **late**. <u>Don't be **late**!</u>
5. Use 4 letters again to spell **over**. <u>The game was **over** at 10:30.</u>
6. Change 1 letter and spell **ever**. <u>Did you **ever** see such an exciting game?</u>
7. Use 4 letters again to spell **vote**. <u>When I am 18, I will be able to **vote**.</u>
8. Add 1 letter and spell **voter**. <u>A person who votes is called a **voter**.</u>
9. Change the first 2 letters and spell **later**. <u>The game ended **later** than we thought it would.</u>
10. Use 6 letters and spell **travel**. <u>I love to **travel**.</u>
11. It's time for the secret word. (Wait 1 minute and then give clues.) <u>We rode the **elevator** to the top floor.</u>

Sort: Display the words on cards in the order they were made and have each word read aloud. Have the related words sorted. Then, have the rhyming words sorted.

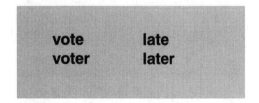

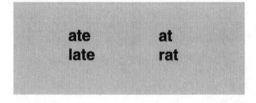

Transfer: Say the following words and have everyone use the rhyming words to spell them:

> that chat gate plate

Word Wall: Call out five of the commonly misspelled words and have everyone chant and write them. Give sentence clues for **their**, **there**, and **they're**. Words: **they**, **were**, **there** ("It is over **there**."), **their** ("**Their** teacher is sick."), **they're** ("**They're** at the mall.").

Lesson 60

Word Wall Words: also editor elevator governors sailor
Suffix for Review: or

Give everyone a copy of the word wall (p. 156) and/or place the words on the classroom word wall.

Review:

Also is added to the word wall because it is a word that is often misspelled. The other words all have the suffix **or.** Sometimes the suffix **or** indicates a person or thing that does something. Have the root words and spelling changes identified and explain the root word/**or** relationship.

editor—edit. <u>**Editors** help writers edit their writing.</u>

sailor—sail. <u>A **sailor** is a person who sails a boat.</u>

governors—govern. <u>The people who govern their states are called **governors**.</u>

elevator—elevate, **e** is dropped. <u>An **elevator** is a machine that lifts you or elevates you to a higher level.</u>

Word Wall:

Call out the five words one at a time and have everyone chant the spelling three times for each word. Next, have everyone write the five words as you give sentence clues.

1. Our room was on the tenth floor so we rode the _____ up.
2. An _____ is a person who helps make your writing easier to read.
3. The _____ from all 50 states had a meeting to discuss the energy crisis.
4. My brother joined the Navy and now he is a _____.
5. I like reading and I _____ like math.

Lesson 61

Letters: i b g h l r t y
Words: big rig rib hit lit girl birth light right bright brightly

Make Words: Distribute the letters and have everyone write the capitals on the back. After each word is made, show the correct spelling. Make sure everyone has each word spelled correctly before doing the next word. Keep the lesson fast paced

1. Take 3 letters and spell **big**. My friend has a really **big** dog.

2. Change 1 letter and spell **rig**. A big truck is called a **rig**.

3. Change 1 letter and spell **rib**. When the girl fell, she broke a **rib**.

4. Use 3 letters to spell **hit**. I hope I get a **hit** in the game tonight.

5. Change 1 letter and spell **lit**. When the power went off, we **lit** some candles.

6. Use 4 letters to spell **girl**. The **girl** won first prize in the contest.

7. Use 5 letters to spell **birth**. My brother got home just in time for the **birth** of his baby.

8. Use 5 letters again to spell **light**. Please turn on the **light**.

9. Change 1 letter and spell **right**. I had all the **right** answers.

10. Add 1 letter and spell **bright**. The sun is very **bright** today.

11. It's time for the secret word. Add your letters to **bright**. (Wait 1 minute and then give clues.) The sun was shining **brightly** this morning.

Sort: Display the words on cards in the order they were made and have each word read aloud. Have the related words sorted. Then, have the rhyming words sorted.

bright	big	right	hit
brightly	rig	bright	lit
		light	

Transfer: Say the following words and have everyone use the rhyming words to spell them:

flight slight twig fight

Word Wall: Have everyone look at the word wall and chant and write the five new words: **also**, **editor**, **sailor**, **governors**, **elevator**.

Lesson 62

Letters: e i d f l n r y
Words: fly fry find line fine file life fried friend friendly

Make Words: Distribute the letters and have everyone write the capitals on the back. After each word is made, show the correct spelling. Make sure everyone has each word spelled correctly before doing the next word. Keep the lesson fast paced.

1. Take 3 letters and spell **fly**. I would love to **fly** an airplane.
2. Change 1 letter and spell **fry**. Should we **fry** the chicken or grill it?
3. Take 4 letters and spell **find**. Help me **find** my lost book.
4. Use 4 letters again to spell **line**. There was a long **line** waiting to get into the game.
5. Change 1 letter and spell **fine**. I am feeling **fine**.
6. Change 1 letter and spell **file**. I am going to keep these in the **file** cabinet.
7. Move the letters around and spell **life**. This is the story of my **life**.
8. Use 5 letters to spell **fried**. Do you like **fried** chicken?
9. Add 1 letter and spell **friend**. My **friend** and I like to play games.
10. It's time for the secret word. Add your letters to **friend** and see what you have. (Wait 1 minute and then give clues.) My dog is very **friendly**.

Sort: Display the words on cards in the order they were made and have each word read aloud. Have the related words sorted. Then, have the rhyming words sorted.

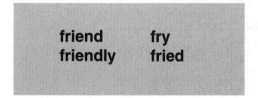

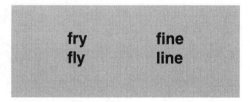

friend	fry		fry	fine
friendly	fried		fly	line

Transfer: Say the following words and have everyone use the rhyming words to spell them:

dine pine shine shy

Word Wall: Call out five root words that can be spelled by dropping suffixes off word wall words. Spelling changes may be needed: **sail**, **govern**, **edit**, **elevate**, **compute**.

Lesson 63

Letters: a o b b l p r y
Words: boy Roy Ray bay lay play baby lobby royal probably

Make Words: Distribute the letters and have everyone write the capitals on the back. After each word is made, show the correct spelling. Make sure everyone has each word spelled correctly before doing the next word. Keep the lesson fast paced.

1. Take 3 letters and spell **boy**. The **boy** won first prize in the contest.
2. Change one letter and spell **Roy**. The boy's name was **Roy** Jones.
3. Change 1 letter and spell **Ray**. Roy's twin brother's name was **Ray** Jones.
4. Change 1 letter and spell **bay**. We went swimming in the **bay**.
5. Change 1 letter and spell **lay**. You can **lay** the dress on the bed.
6. Add 1 letter and spell **play**. Do you know how to **play** the guitar?
7. Use 4 letters again to spell **baby**. How old is the **baby**?
8. Use 5 letters to spell **lobby**. We met in the **lobby** of the hotel.
9. Use 5 letters again to spell **royal**. The prince was a member of the **royal** family.
10. It's time for the secret word. (Wait 1 minute and then give clues.) I'm not sure I can go but I **probably** can.

Sort: Display the words on cards in the order they were made and have each word read aloud. Have the rhyming words sorted.

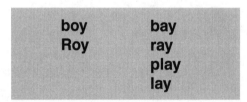

boy	bay
Roy	ray
	play
	lay

Transfer: Say the following words and have everyone use the rhyming words to spell them:

joy toy tray stray

Word Wall: Call out five words that can be spelled by combining root words with other suffixes. Spelling changes may be needed: **governed**, **editing**, **sailed**, **elevates**, **computing**.

Lesson 64

Letters: a e l l r y
Words: lay Ray are ear year real relay early layer rally really

Make Words: Distribute the letters and have everyone write the capitals on the back. After each word is made, show the correct spelling. Make sure everyone has each word spelled correctly before doing the next word. Keep the lesson fast paced.

1. Use 3 letters to spell **lay**. This afternoon I am going to **lay** back and relax.
2. Change 1 letter and spell **Ray**. Uncle **Ray** is taking me to the game tomorrow.
3. Use 3 letters to spell **are**. Where **are** you going?
4. Move the letters around and spell **ear**. I got stung on the **ear**.
5. Add 1 letter and spell **year**. Next **year**, I will go to a new school.
6. Use 4 letters again to spell **real**. Is that a **real** gold watch?
7. Use 5 letters to spell **relay**. I like to run **relay** races.
8. Move the letters around and spell **early**. I got up very **early** this morning.
9. Move the letters again and spell **layer**. She baked a chocolate **layer** cake.
10. Use 5 letters again to spell **rally**. We had a **rally** before the big game.
11. Add 1 letter to **rally** and you will have the secret word. (Give clues after one minute.)
    That was a **really** exciting game.

Sort: Display the words on cards in the order they were made and have each word read aloud. Have the related words sorted. Then, have the rhyming words sorted.

real
really

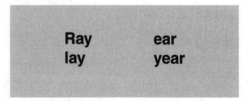

Ray   ear
lay   year

Transfer: Say the following words and have everyone use the rhyming words to spell them:

stay stray spray fear

Word Wall: Call out five of the commonly misspelled words. Have everyone chant and write the words: **are**, **our**, **also**, **have**, **went**.

Lesson 65

Word Wall Words: brightly friendly probably really right
Suffix for Review: ly

Give everyone a copy of the word wall (p.157) and/or place the words on the classroom word wall.

Review:

Right is added to the word wall because it is a word that is often confused with **write**. The other words all have the suffix **ly**. Adding the suffix **ly** to a root word changes how that word is used in sentences. Have the root words and spelling changes identified and explain the root word/**ly** relationship.

brightly—bright. <u>When something is bright, we say it shines **brightly**.</u>

friendly—friend. <u>A person who is **friendly** acts like you are her friend.</u>

probably—probable drop **le**, add **ly**. <u>If it is probable that something will happen, we say it will **probably** happen.</u>

really—real. <u>When we talk about a real, true event, we can say it **really** happened. **Really** can also mean "very." That was a **really** good movie.</u>

Word Wall:

Call out the five words one at a time and have everyone chant the spelling three times for each word. Next, have everyone write the five words as you give sentence clues.

1. I am not sure I can go, but I _____ can.

2. There was not a cloud in the sky and the sun shone very _____.

3. That dog is very _____ and wants to lick everyone.

4. I was there when the argument started and I know what _____ happened.

5. The opposite of wrong is _____.

Lessons 66-70
Suffixes: ful; less

Lesson 66

Letters: a e u c f l r
Words: ear car far ace race care cure fuel cruel careful

Make Words: Distribute the letters and have everyone write the capitals on the back. After each word is made, show the correct spelling. Make sure everyone has each word spelled correctly before doing the next word. Keep the lesson fast paced.

1. Take 3 letters and spell **ear**. <u>My grandpa can't hear with his left **ear**.</u>

2. Change 1 letter and spell **car**. <u>We bought a new **car**.</u>

3. Change 1 letter and spell **far**. <u>How **far** is it to the mountains?</u>

4. Use 3 letters to spell **ace**. <u>She dealt me the **ace** of spades and the **ace** of clubs.</u>

5. Add 1 letter and spell **race**. <u>Who won the **race**?</u>

6. Move the letters around and spell **care**. <u>I don't **care** where we go to eat.</u>

7. Change 1 letter and spell **cure**. <u>I hope they find a **cure** for cancer.</u>

8. Use 4 letters again to spell **fuel**. <u>The plane had to land and get more **fuel**.</u>

9. Take off the **f** and add 2 letters to spell **cruel**. <u>Calling people names is unkind and **cruel**.</u>

10. It's time for the secret word. Add your letters to a word we already made. (Wait 1 minute and then give clues.) <u>Be **careful** crossing the busy street.</u>

Sort: Display the words on cards in the order they were made and have each word read aloud. Have the related words sorted. Then, have the rhyming words sorted.

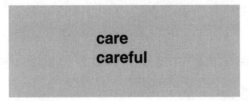

care
careful

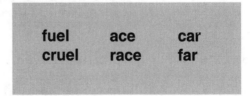

fuel   ace   car
cruel   race   far

Transfer: Say the following words and have everyone use the rhyming words to spell them:

face place duel scar

Word Wall: Have everyone look at the word wall and chant and write the five new words: **right, really, probably, friendly, brightly.**

Letters: a e i u u b f l t
Words: bat bit but bet belt felt left lift able table beautiful

Make Words: Distribute the letters and have everyone write the capitals on the back. After each word is made, show the correct spelling. Make sure everyone has each word spelled correctly before doing the next word. Keep the lesson fast paced.

1. Use 3 letters to spell **bat**. It is my turn at **bat**.

2. Change 1 letter and spell **bit**. It hurt when I **bit** my tongue.

3. Change 1 letter and spell **but**. I wanted to go **but** my dad said I couldn't.

4. Change 1 letter and spell **bet**. I **bet** I can throw the ball farther than you can.

5. Add 1 letter and spell **belt**. I bought a new **belt**.

6. Change 1 letter and spell **felt**. The baby was crying and her head **felt** very hot.

7. Move the letters around and spell **left**. Are there any cookies **left**?

8. Change 1 letter and spell **lift**. The workers used a crane to **lift** the heavy blocks.

9. Use 4 letters again to spell **able**. My grandpa was not **able** to visit last weekend.

10. Add 1 letter and spell **table**. Let's sit at that **table**.

11. It's time for the secret word. (Wait 1 minute and then give clues.) The bride was **beautiful**.

Sort: Display the words on cards in the order they were made and have each word read aloud. Have the rhyming words sorted.

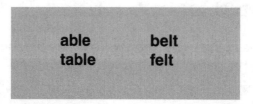

able	belt
table	felt

Transfer: Say the following words and have everyone use the rhyming words to spell them:

melt cable stable pelt

Word Wall: Call out five root words that can be spelled by dropping suffixes off word wall words. Spelling changes may be needed: **real**, **friend**, **bright**, **probable**, **govern**.

Lesson 68

Letters: e e h l l p s s
Words: see seep less help sell shell spell sleep sheep helpless

Make Words: Distribute the letters and have everyone write the capitals on the back. After each word is made, show the correct spelling. Make sure everyone has each word spelled correctly before doing the next word. Keep the lesson fast paced.

1. Take 3 letters and spell **see**. Did you **see** the movie?

2. Add 1 letter and spell **seep**. When it rains hard, the water will **seep** into the basement.

3. Use 4 letters again to spell **less**. I helped with the work but I got paid **less** than my brother.

4. Use 4 letters again to spell **help**. I am not going to **help** next time.

5. Use 4 letters again to spell **sell**. I am going to **sell** my old bike.

6. Add 1 letter and spell **shell**. The turtle poked his head out of his **shell**.

7. Change 1 letter and spell **spell**. Use your letters to spell "**spell**."

8. Use 5 letters again to spell **sleep**. Sometimes, I **sleep** in my tent.

9. Change 1 letter and spell **sheep**. We saw the **sheep** in the field.

10. Combine 2 of the words we already made and you will have the secret word. (After 1 minute, give clues.) The baby kitten was **helpless**.

Sort: Display the words on cards in the order they were made and have each word read aloud. Have the related words sorted. Then, have the rhyming words sorted.

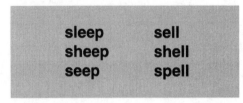

Transfer: Say the following words and have everyone use the rhyming words to spell them:

sweep swell well weep

Word Wall: Call out five words that can be spelled by combining root words with **ly**. Spelling changes may be needed: **easily**, **heavily**, **nationally**, **musically**, **healthily**.

Lesson 69

Make Words: Distribute the letters and have everyone write the capitals on the back. After each word is made, show the correct spelling. Make sure everyone has each word spelled correctly before doing the next word. Keep the lesson fast paced.

1. Use 4 letters to spell **less**. <u>I am going to buy these jeans because they cost **less**</u>.
2. Use 4 letters again to spell **with**. <u>Will you go to the mall **with** me?</u>
3. Use 4 letters again to spell **wise**. <u>Why do they say an owl is **wise**?</u>
4. Use 4 letters again to spell **heel**. <u>I have a wart on the **heel** of my foot.</u>
5. Add 1 letter and spell **wheel**. <u>We put a new tire on the front **wheel**.</u>
6. Use 5 letters again to spell **sweet**. <u>I like to eat **sweet** things.</u>
7. Change 1 letter and spell **sheet**. <u>Can I borrow a **sheet** of paper?</u>
8. Use 5 letters again to spell **eight**. <u>My mom said I could invite **eight** people to my party.</u>
9. Add 1 letter and spell **weight**. <u>My **weight** is 68 pounds.</u>
10. Add your letters to **weight** and you will have the secret word. (After 1 minute, give clues.) <u>When you go up in space, you are **weightless**.</u>

Sort: Display the words on cards in the order they were made and have each word read aloud. Have the related words sorted. Then, have the rhyming words sorted.

weight		
weightless		

eight	**heel**	**sweet**
weight	**wheel**	**sheet**

Transfer: Say the following words and have everyone use the rhyming words to spell them:

greet steel feel feet

Word Wall: Call out five words that can be spelled by combining root words with either **er** or **est**. Spelling changes may be needed: **brighter**, **brightest**, **friendlier**, **friendliest**, **healthier**.

Lesson 70

Word Wall Words: beautiful careful helpless weightless with
Suffixes for Review: full; less

Give everyone a copy of the word wall (p. 158) and/or place the words on the classroom word wall.

Review:

With is added to the word wall because it is a word that is often misspelled. The other words all have the suffix **ful** or **less**. Words that end in **ful** and **less** are often opposites. A person who takes care in doing things is **careful**; a person who doesn't is **careless**. A person who helps you is **helpful** and a person who can't help is **helpless**. Have the root words and spelling changes identified and have each word used in a sentence.

beautiful—beauty, **y** changes to **i**. When something has a lot of beauty, we say it is **beautiful**.

careful—care. It is important to be **careful** when crossing the street.

helpless—help. The newborn rabbit was **helpless** and had to be fed and protected.

weightless—weight. In space, things have no weight and we say they are **weightless**.

Word Wall:

Call out the five words one at a time and have everyone chant the spelling three times for each word. Next, have everyone write the five words as you give sentence clues.

1. The astronaut had to get used to being _____.

2. After she broke both arms in a car accident, my aunt was _____.

3. Be _____ that you don't burn yourself on the hot stove.

4. The flowers blooming in the garden are _____.

5. I went to the mall _____ my cousin.

Lesson 71

Letters: a e d k n r s s
Words: ask end send sand dark rake snake sneak asked darkness

Make Words: Distribute the letters and have everyone write the capitals on the back. After each word is made, show the correct spelling. Make sure everyone has each word spelled correctly before doing the next word. Keep the lesson fast paced.

1. Take 3 letters and spell **ask**. <u>Does anyone want to **ask** a question?</u>

2. Take 3 letters and spell **end**. <u>I am almost to the **end** of my book.</u>

3. Add 1 letter and spell **send**. <u>I am going to **send** her a birthday card.</u>

4. Change 1 letter and spell **sand**. <u>I like to dig in the **sand**.</u>

5. Use 4 letters again to spell **dark**. <u>It is very **dark** in my bedroom.</u>

6. Use 4 letters again to spell **rake**. <u>Will you help me **rake** the leaves?</u>

7. Take the **r** off and add 1 letter to spell **snake**. <u>We saw a **snake** in the garden.</u>

8. Move the letters around and spell **sneak**. <u>We tried to **sneak** up on him.</u>

9. Use 5 letters to spell **asked**. <u>I **asked** my mom if my friend could spend the night.</u>

10. It's time for the secret word. Add your letters to a word we already made. (Wait 1 minute and then give clues.) <u>When the power went out, we were in complete **darkness**.</u>

Sort: Display the words on cards in the order they were made and have each word read aloud. Have the related words sorted. Then, have the rhyming words sorted.

dark	ask
darkness	asked

end	rake
send	snake

Transfer: Say the following words and have everyone use the rhyming words to spell them:

shake wake bake bend

Word Wall: Have everyone look at the word wall and chant and write the five new words: **with**, **beautiful**, **careful**, **weightless**, **helpless**.

Lesson 72

Letters: a e d n s s s
Words: ad Ed Ned den end and sad sand Dean sadness

Make Words: Distribute the letters and have everyone write the capitals on the back. After each word is made, show the correct spelling. Make sure everyone has each word spelled correctly before doing the next word. Keep the lesson fast paced.

1. Take 2 letters and spell **ad**. We put an **ad** in the paper to try to find our lost dog.
2. Change 1 letter and spell **Ed**. A man named **Ed** found our dog and called us.
3. Add 1 letter and spell **Ned**. **Ned** works at Wal-Mart.
4. Move the letters around and spell **den**. Our TV is in the **den**.
5. Move the letters again and spell **end**. On Friday, I couldn't wait for school to **end**.
6. Change 1 letter and spell **and**. We had popcorn **and** juice for a snack.
7. Take 3 letters and spell **sad**. Do you ever feel **sad**?
8. Add 1 letter and spell **sand**. I lost my quarter in the **sand**.
9. Use 4 letters again to spell **Dean**. My aunt named her baby **Dean**.
10. It's time for the secret word. Add your letters to a word we already made. (Wait 1 minute and then give clues.) **Sadness** filled the room when the teacher read about the dog dying.

Sort: Display the words on cards in the order they were made and have each word read aloud. Have the related words sorted. Then, have the rhyming words sorted.

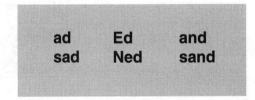

sad		
sadness		

ad	Ed	and
sad	Ned	sand

Transfer: Say the following words and have everyone use the rhyming words to spell them:

bed had brand hand

Word Wall: Call out five root words that can be spelled by dropping suffixes off word wall words. Spelling changes may be needed: **help**, **care**, **weight**, **weigh**, **beauty**.

Lesson 73

Letters: a e i h n p p s s
Words: ape sip snip ship shape spies ashes happen pansies happiness

Make Words: Distribute the letters and have everyone write the capitals on the back. After each word is made, show the correct spelling. Make sure everyone has each word spelled correctly before doing the next word. Keep the lesson fast paced.

1. Take 3 letters and spell **ape**. A gorilla is an **ape**.

2. Take 3 letters and spell **sip**. Can I have a **sip** of your soda?

3. Add 1 letter and spell **snip**. I cut a little **snip** off my hair.

4. Change 1 letter and spell **ship**. They sailed to America on a large **ship**.

5. Use 5 letters to spell **shape**. A triangle is a **shape** with three sides.

6. Use 5 letters again to spell **spies**. They arrested the **spies** and put them in jail.

7. Use 5 letters again to spell **ashes**. Dad cleaned the **ashes** out of the fireplace.

8. Use 6 letters to spell **happen**. I don't know how that can **happen**.

9. Use 7 letters to spell **pansies**. **Pansies** are flowers that grow in many colors.

10. It's time for the secret word. (Wait 1 minute and then give clues.) Our whole family was filled with **happiness** when our puppy was found.

Sort: Display the words on cards in the order they were made and have each word read aloud. Have the rhyming words sorted.

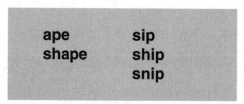

ape	sip
shape	ship
	snip

Transfer: Say the following words and have everyone use the rhyming words to spell them:

grape drape strip clip

Word Wall: Call out five words that can be spelled by combining root words with **ly**. Spelling changes may be needed: **carefully, beautifully, nationally, easily, helplessly.**

Letters: a e e i d n r s s
Words: sad said seed need idea rain drain rained easier readiness

Make Words: Distribute the letters and have everyone write the capitals on the back. After each word is made, show the correct spelling. Make sure everyone has each word spelled correctly before doing the next word. Keep the lesson fast paced.

1. Take 3 letters and spell **sad**. Why do you look so **sad**?

2. Add 1 letter and spell **said**. I couldn't hear what he **said**.

3. Use 4 letters again to spell **seed**. An acorn is the **seed** for an oak tree.

4. Change 1 letter and spell **need**. Does anyone **need** help?

5. Use 4 letters again to spell **idea**. That was a very good **idea**.

6. Use 4 letters again to spell **rain**. Before the game ended, it started to **rain**.

7. Add 1 letter and spell **drain**. The plumber had to clean out the **drain**.

8. Use 6 letters to spell **rained**. It **rained** all night.

9. Use 6 letters to spell **easier**. The test this week was **easier** than last week's test.

10. It's time for the secret word. (Wait 1 minute and then give clues.) People along the coast were in a state of **readiness** waiting for the hurricane.

Sort: Display the words on cards in the order they were made and have each word read aloud. Have the related words sorted. Then, have the rhyming words sorted.

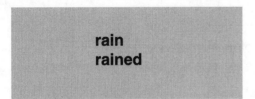

rain
rained

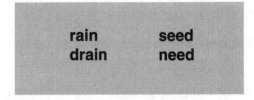

rain   seed
drain   need

Transfer: Say the following words and have everyone use the rhyming words to spell them:

weed brain breed strain

Word Wall: Call out five words that can be spelled by combining root words with **ful** or **less**. Spelling changes may be needed: **careless, helpful, watchful, friendless, frightful**.

Lesson 75

Word Wall Words: darkness happiness readiness sadness said
Suffix for Review: ness

Give everyone a copy of the word wall (p. 159) and/or place the words on the classroom word wall.

Review:

Said is added to the word wall because it is a word that is often misspelled. The other words all have the suffix **ness**. Adding the suffix **ness** to a root word changes the how that word is used in sentences. Have the root words and spelling changes identified and have each word used in a sentence.

darkness—dark. At camp, we sat in the **darkness** and told ghost stories.

happiness—happy, **y** changes to **i**. The new baby brought **happiness** to everyone in the family.

readiness—ready, **y** changes to **i**. We waited in **readiness** for the storm to arrive.

sadness—sad. The room was filled with **sadness** when we heard that we lost the game.

Word Wall:

Call out the five words one at a time and have everyone chant the spelling three times for each word. Next, have everyone write the five words as you give sentence clues.

1. The opposite of sadness is _____.

2. The opposite of happiness is _____.

3. The lights went out and the room was suddenly plunged into complete _____.

4. We all waited in _____ for the arrival of the guest of honor.

5. It was noisy and I couldn't hear what the speaker _____.

Lesson 76

Letters: e i u b d l r
Words: bed red rid ride rude rule bride build builder rebuild

Make Words: Distribute the letters and have everyone write the capitals on the back. After each word is made, show the correct spelling. Make sure everyone has each word spelled correctly before doing the next word. Keep the lesson fast paced.

1. Take 3 letters and spell **bed**. <u>What time did you go to **bed**?</u>

2. Change 1 letter and spell **red**. <u>My new bike is **red**.</u>

3. Change 1 letter and spell **rid**. <u>I got **rid** of all the toys I don't play with anymore.</u>

4. Add 1 letter and spell **ride**. <u>We got a **ride** to school.</u>

5. Change 1 letter and spell **rude**. <u>It is **rude** to interrupt when someone else is talking.</u>

6. Change 1 letter and spell **rule**. <u>"No fighting" is an important **rule**.</u>

7. Use 5 letters to spell **bride**. <u>The **bride** arrived at the wedding late.</u>

8. Use 5 letters again to spell **build**. <u>I like to **build** things.</u>

9. There are 2 secret words today. Add your letters to **build** and see if you can figure them out. (After 1 minute, give some clues.) <u>After the fire, the **builder** had to **rebuild** the house.</u>

Sort: Display the words on cards in the order they were made and have each word read aloud. Have the related words sorted. Then, have the rhyming words sorted.

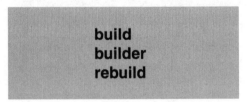

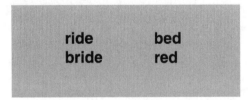

Transfer: Say the following words and have everyone use the rhyming words to spell them:

wide wed stride glide

Word Wall: Have everyone look at the word wall and chant and write the five new words: **said**, **happiness**, **sadness**, **darkness**, **readiness**.

Lesson 77

Letters: e e i d f l l r
Words: fee free fill fire fired fried drill filled refill refilled

Make Words: Distribute the letters and have everyone write the capitals on the back. After each word is made, show the correct spelling. Make sure everyone has each word spelled correctly before doing the next word. Keep the lesson fast paced.

1. Take 3 letters and spell **fee**. <u>The entry **fee** was $5.00.</u>

2. Add 1 letter and spell **free**. <u>I didn't have to pay because I won a **free** pass.</u>

3. Use 4 letters again to spell **fill**. <u>Before our trip, we will **fill** up the gas tank.</u>

4. Use 4 letters again to spell **fire**. <u>Do you know what caused the **fire**?</u>

5. Add 1 letter and spell **fired**. <u>The man got **fired** because he was always late for work.</u>

6. Move the letters around and spell **fried**. <u>We caught some fish and then we **fried** them in oil.</u>

7. Use 5 letters again to spell **drill**. <u>I hate it when the dentist has to **drill** my teeth.</u>

8. Use 6 letters to spell **filled**. <u>I had two teeth **filled** last week.</u>

9. Use 6 letters to spell **refill**. <u>May I please have a **refill** on my Coke?</u>

10. It's time for the secret word. Add your letters to **refill**. (Wait 1 minute and then give clues.) <u>They **refilled** my drink twice.</u>

Sort: Display the words on cards in the order they were made and have each word read aloud. Have the related words sorted. Then, have the rhyming words sorted.

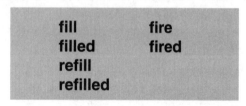

fill	fire
filled	fired
refill	
refilled	

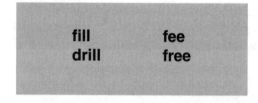

fill	fee
drill	free

Transfer: Say the following words and have everyone use the rhyming words to spell them:

> **tree still skill shrill**

Word Wall: Call out five root words that can be spelled by dropping suffixes off word wall words. Spelling changes may be needed: **happy, sad, ready, dark, beauty.**

Lesson 78

Letters: a e e c l p r
Words: are ace ape pal lap clap cape pace race place replace

Make Words: Distribute the letters and have everyone write the capitals on the back. After each word is made, show the correct spelling. Make sure everyone has each word spelled correctly before doing the next word. Keep the lesson fast paced.

1. Take 3 letters and spell **are**. Where **are** we going?

2. Change 1 letter and spell **ace**. I hope I "**ace**" the test.

3. Change 1 letter and spell **ape**. A chimpanzee is a small **ape**.

4. Use 3 letters to spell **pal**. I wrote a letter to my pen **pal**.

5. Move the letters around and spell **lap**. I held the baby in my **lap**.

6. Add 1 letter and spell **clap**. The baby is learning to **clap**.

7. Use 4 letters again to spell **cape**. Superman wore a **cape**.

8. Move the letters around and spell **pace**. The **pace** car went around the track first.

9. Change 1 letter and spell **race**. It was an exciting **race**.

10. Take the **r** off and add 2 letters to spell **place**. This is my **place**.

11. It's time for the secret word. Add your letters to **place**. (Wait 1 minute and then give clues.) I broke a glass but I bought a new one to **replace** it.

Sort: Display the words on cards in the order they were made and have each word read aloud. Have the related words sorted. Then, have the rhyming words sorted.

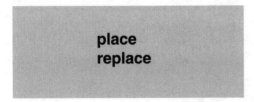

place
replace

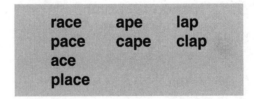

race   ape   lap
pace   cape clap
ace
place

Transfer: Say the following words and have everyone use the rhyming words to spell them:

shape slap trace grape

Word Wall: Call out five word wall words which show the **y** to **i** spelling change: **happiness, readiness, beautiful, countries, heavier.**

Lesson 79

Letters: a e e c d l l r
Words: all ace race call lead clear leader caller recall cleared recalled

Make Words: Distribute the letters and have everyone write the capitals on the back. After each word is made, show the correct spelling. Make sure everyone has each word spelled correctly before doing the next word. Keep the lesson fast paced.

1. Use 3 letters to spell **all**. We are **all** going on the trip.

2. Use 3 letters to spell **ace**. The **ace** is the highest card.

3. Add 1 letter and spell **race**. Let's have a **race**.

4. Use 4 letters again to spell **call**. What time should I **call** you?

5. Use 4 letters again to spell **lead**. I like to **lead** the line.

6. Use 5 letters to spell **clear**. It was a cold, **clear** day.

7. Use 6 letters to spell **leader**. The person who leads the line is the **leader**.

8. Use 6 letters to spell **caller**. Do you have **caller** ID on your phone?

9. Move the letters around and spell **recall**. If a product is defective, they will **recall** it.

10. Use 7 letters to spell **cleared**. We **cleared** the table after dinner.

11. Add your letters to a word we already made and you will have the secret word. (Give clues after 1 minute.) Our new car was **recalled** because the tires were faulty.

Sort: Display the words on cards in the order they were made and have each word read aloud. Have the related words sorted. Then, have the rhyming words sorted.

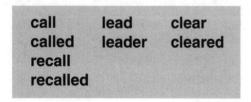

call	lead	clear
called	leader	cleared
recall		
recalled		

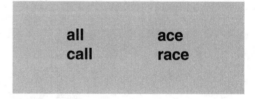

all	ace
call	race

Transfer: Say the following words and have everyone use the rhyming words to spell them:

stall space face fall

Word Wall: Call out the five contractions on the word wall: **wouldn't, shouldn't, don't, doesn't, they're.** Have the contractions chanted and written.

Lesson 80

Word Wall Words: builder rebuild refilled recalled replace
Prefix for Review: re

Give everyone a copy of the word wall (p. 160) and/or place the words on the classroom word wall.

Review:

Builder is added to the word wall because it is another word in which the **er** suffix indicates a person who does something. A builder builds. The other words all have the prefix **re**. The prefix **re** often adds the meaning of "again" or "back" to a word. When you rebuild or refill something, you build or fill it again. When you recall or replace something, you call it back or place it back. Have the root words, prefixes, and suffixes identified and have each word used in a sentence.

builder—build **er**. <u>The **builder** built the house.</u>

rebuild—**re** build. <u>The house burned down and we had to **rebuild** it.</u>

refilled—**re** fill ed. <u>The waitress **refilled** our drinks.</u>

recalled—**re** call ed. <u>The defective car seats were all **recalled**.</u>

replace—**re** place. <u>I will **replace** the paper I borrowed.</u>

Word Wall:

Call out the five words one at a time and have everyone chant the spelling three times for each word. Next, have everyone write the five words as you give sentence clues.

1. After the robbery, we had to _____ all the locks.

2. We were all thirsty and _____ our drinks several times.

3. The toys were _____ because they had parts that could break off and choke little children.

4. The tower I was building fell down and now I have to _____ it.

5. I am a good _____.

Lesson 81

Letters: a e e u b n n t
Words: at bat but nut eat neat beat eaten beaten unbeaten

Make Words: Distribute the letters and have everyone write the capitals on the back. After each word is made, show the correct spelling. Make sure everyone has each word spelled correctly before doing the next word. Keep the lesson fast paced.

1. Take 2 letters and spell **at**. We are all meeting **at** the mall.

2. Add 1 letter and spell **bat**. A **bat** is a mammal with wings.

3. Change 1 letter and spell **but**. I have never seen a bat **but** I would like to.

4. Change 1 letter and spell **nut**. The squirrel was eating a **nut**.

5. Use 3 letters to spell **eat**. Bats **eat** insects.

6. Add 1 letter and spell **neat**. I like to keep my room clean and **neat**.

7. Change 1 letter and spell **beat**. My favorite team **beat** the other team.

8. Use 5 letters to spell **eaten**. We have **eaten** all the cookies.

9. Add 1 letter and spell **beaten**. Our team has **beaten** them in the last five games.

10. Add your letters to **beaten** and you will have the secret word. (Give clues after 1 minute.) Our team was the only team that didn't lose a game and ended the season **unbeaten**.

Sort: Display the words on cards in the order they were made and have each word read aloud. Have the related words sorted. Then, have the rhyming words sorted.

beat	eat
beaten	eaten
unbeaten	

eat	but	eaten	at
beat	nut	beaten	bat
neat			

Transfer: Say the following words and have everyone use the rhyming words to spell them:

shut treat flat wheat

Word Wall: Have everyone look at the word wall and chant and write the five new words: **rebuild, builder, refilled, recalled, replace.**

Lesson 82

Letters: e e e u c d n p t x
Words: pet net next dune tune tuned except expect expected unexpected

Make Words: Distribute the letters and have everyone write the capitals on the back. After each word is made, show the correct spelling. Make sure everyone has each word spelled correctly before doing the next word. Keep the lesson fast paced.

1. Take 3 letters and spell **pet**. <u>I have a goldfish for a **pet**.</u>

2. Change 1 letter and spell **net**. <u>We use a **net** to clean out the fish tank.</u>

3. Add 1 letter and spell **next**. <u>I sat **next** to my friend on the bus.</u>

4. Take 4 letters and spell **dune**. <u>Our favorite beach has a large sand **dune**.</u>

5. Change 1 letter and spell **tune**. <u>We called someone to come and **tune** our piano.</u>

6. Add 1 letter and spell **tuned**. <u>The piano hadn't ever been **tuned** before.</u>

7. Use 6 letters to spell **except**. <u>Everyone came to the party **except** my aunt.</u>

8. Move the letters around and spell **expect**. <u>We did not **expect** her to come because she lives far away.</u>

9. Add 2 letters and spell **expected**. <u>We **expected** all the other relatives to come.</u>

10. Add your letters to **expected** and you will have the secret word. (Give clues after 1 minute.) <u>The bike my aunt sent me for my birthday was **unexpected**!</u>

Sort: Display the words on cards in the order they were made and have each word read aloud. Have the related words sorted. Then, have the rhyming words sorted.

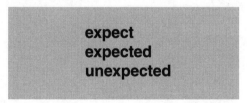

expect
expected
unexpected

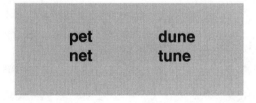

pet   dune
net   tune

Transfer: Say the following words and have everyone use the rhyming words to spell them:

June prune wet jet

Word Wall: Call out five root words that can be spelled by dropping suffixes off word wall words: **build, call, fill, place, govern**.

Lesson 83

Letters: a e e i d g r s
Words: ride side said seed greed agree agreed erased easier disagree

Make Words: Distribute the letters and have everyone write the capitals on the back. After each word is made, show the correct spelling. Make sure everyone has each word spelled correctly before doing the next word. Keep the lesson fast paced.

1. Take 4 letters and spell **ride**. I let my friends **ride** my bike.

2. Change 1 letter and spell **side**. After the race, I had a pain in my **side**.

3. Take 4 letters and spell **said**. My mom **said** I should drink lots of water.

4. Take 4 letters and spell **seed**. I swallowed a watermelon **seed**.

5. Remove the **s** and add 2 letters to spell **greed**. One look at the gold filled the pirate with **greed**.

6. Use 5 letters again to spell **agree**. My sister and I could not **agree** on what to play.

7. Add 1 letter and spell **agreed**. Finally we **agreed** to take turns.

8. Use 6 letters again to spell **erased**. I **erased** the board.

9. Use 6 letters again to spell **easier**. Skating is **easier** than I thought it would be.

10. It's time for the secret word. Add your letters to a word we already made. (Wait 1 minute and then give clues.) My brother and I **disagree** about which teams we like.

Sort: Display the words on cards in the order they were made and have each word read aloud. Have the related words sorted. Then, have the rhyming words sorted.

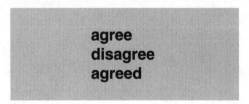

agree
disagree
agreed

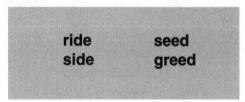

ride   seed
side   greed

Transfer: Say the following words and have everyone use the rhyming words to spell them:

slide weed speed bleed

Word Wall: Call out five **ing** words that can be spelled by using word wall words. Spelling changes may be needed: **building**, **filling**, **placing**, **calling**, **helping**.

Lesson 84

Letters: a a e i d p p r s
Words: sip rip drip dear spear spider sipped ripped appear disappear

Make Words: Distribute the letters and have everyone write the capitals on the back. After each word is made, show the correct spelling. Make sure everyone has each word spelled correctly before doing the next word. Keep the lesson fast paced.

1. Take 3 letters and spell **sip**. <u>Can I have a **sip** of your drink to see if I like it?</u>

2. Change 1 letter and spell **rip**. <u>These jeans have a **rip** in them.</u>

3. Add 1 letter and spell **drip**. <u>Turn the faucet off tight so the water won't **drip**.</u>

4. Take 4 letters and spell **dear**. <u>My grandma is always saying, "Oh **dear**!"</u>

5. Remove the **d** and add 2 letters to spell **spear**. <u>The warrior hunted with a **spear**.</u>

6. Use 6 letters to spell **spider**. <u>A **spider** traps insects in her web.</u>

7. Use 6 letters again to spell **sipped**. <u>They talked and **sipped** their tea.</u>

8. Change 1 letter and spell **ripped**. <u>He fell and **ripped** his shirt.</u>

9. Use 6 letters again to spell **appear**. <u>We sat very quietly hoping the deer would **appear**.</u>

10. Add your letters to **appear** and you will have the secret word. (Give clues after 1 minute.) <u>The opposite of appear is **disappear**.</u>

Sort: Display the words on cards in the order they were made and have each word read aloud. Have the related words sorted. Then, have the rhyming words sorted.

appear	sip	rip
disappear	sipped	ripped

dip	dear	ripped
sip	spear	sipped
drip		

Transfer: Say the following words and have everyone use the rhyming words to spell them:

> **dipped dripped clear trip**

Word Wall: Call out five compound words that can be spelled by using word wall words: **anyone, someone, everything, anything, somewhere.**

Lesson 85

Word Wall Words: disagree disappear except unbeaten unexpected
Prefixes for Review: dis; un

Give everyone a copy of the word wall (p. 161) and/or place the words on the classroom word wall.

Review:

Except is added to the word wall because it is often misspelled. The other words begin with the prefix **dis** or **un**. The prefixes **dis** and **un** often change the meaning of the root word to an opposite meaning. The opposite of agree is **disagree**. The opposite of beaten in **unbeaten**. Have the root words, prefixes, suffixes, and opposites identified.

disagree—dis agree. <u>The opposite of agree is **disagree**.</u>

disappeared—dis appear ed. <u>The opposite of appeared is **disappeared**.</u>

unbeaten—un beat en. <u>The opposite of beaten is **unbeaten**.</u>

unexpected—un expect ed. <u>The opposite of expected is **unexpected**.</u>

Word Wall:

Call out the five words one at a time and have everyone chant the spelling three times for each word. Next, have everyone write the five words as you give sentence clues.

1. The deer looked up and saw me and quickly _____.

2. Our team tied one game but we were _____ in the rest of the games.

3. We all like to eat out but we _____ about which restaurant to go to.

4. My grandparents coming to my birthday party was completely _____.

5. Everyone knew they were coming _____ me.

Lessons 86-90
Prefixes: in; im

Lesson 86

Letters: e i i o b l m p s s
Words: mess less loss boss pile mile miles smile simple possible impossible

Make Words: Distribute the letters and have everyone write the capitals on the back. After each word is made, show the correct spelling. Make sure everyone has each word spelled correctly before doing the next word. Keep the lesson fast paced.

1. Take 4 letters and spell **mess**. This room is a **mess**!

2. Change 1 letter and spell **less**. Six is **less** than ten.

3. Change 1 letter and spell **loss**. Last night's game was our first **loss** of the season.

4. Change 1 letter and spell **boss**. My uncle is the **boss** at the construction company.

5. Take 4 letters and spell **pile**. The football players all went down in a **pile**.

6. Change 1 letter and spell **mile**. We run a **mile** around the track.

7. Add 1 letter and spell **miles**. Marathon runners run 26 **miles**.

8. Move the letters around and spell **smile**. The winner had a big **smile** on her face.

9. Take 6 letters and spell **simple**. Fixing the bike was a **simple** job.

10. Take 8 letters and spell **possible**. It is **possible** to get all A's on your report card but you have to work really hard.

11. Add your letters to **possible** and you will have the secret word. (Give clues after 1 minute.) Getting all my homework done tonight is going to be **impossible**.

Sort: Display the words on cards in the order they were made and have each word read aloud. Have the related words sorted. Then, have the rhyming words sorted.

possible	mile
impossible	miles

mess	loss	mile
less	boss	pile
		smile

Transfer: Say the following words and have everyone use the rhyming words to spell them:

cross bless file dress

Word Wall: Have everyone look at the word wall and chant and write the five new words: **except**, **disappear**, **unexpected**, **unbeaten**, **disagree**.

Lesson 87

Letters: a e i u m m r t
Words: eat ate rate mate meat team tame time timer mature immature

Make Words: Distribute the letters and have everyone write the capitals on the back. After each word is made, show the correct spelling. Make sure everyone has each word spelled correctly before doing the next word. Keep the lesson fast paced.

1. Take 3 letters and spell **eat**. <u>What do you like to **eat**</u>?

2. Move the letters around and spell **ate**. <u>Who **ate** all the cookies?</u>

3. Add 1 letter and spell **rate**. <u>How would you **rate** that movie?</u>

4. Change 1 letter and spell **mate**. <u>The bird was singing to attract a **mate**.</u>

5. Move the letters around and spell **meat**. <u>Vegetarians do not eat **meat**.</u>

6. Move the letters again and spell **team**. <u>Our football **team** won the championship.</u>

7. Move the letters again and spell **tame**. <u>The opposite of wild is **tame**.</u>

8. Change 1 letter and spell **time**. <u>What **time** is it?</u>

9. Add 1 letter and spell **timer**. <u>I put the cake in the oven and set the **timer**.</u>

10. Take 6 letters and spell **mature**. <u>People say I am very **mature** for my age.</u>

11. Add your letters to **mature** and you will have the secret word. (Give clues after 1 minute.) <u>My brother does not act his age and is very **immature**.</u>

Sort: Display the words on cards in the order they were made and have each word read aloud. Have the related words sorted. Then, have the rhyming words sorted.

mature	time		eat	ate
immature	timer		meat	rate
				mate

Transfer: Say the following words and have everyone use the rhyming words to spell them:

state   treat   cheat   slate

Word Wall: Call out five word wall words that end in **ed: unexpected, married, grabbed, squirted, floated**.

Lesson 88

Letters: e i o c c n r r t
Words: ice nice rent cent into torn corn corner concert correct incorrect

Make Words: Distribute the letters and have everyone write the capitals on the back. After each word is made, show the correct spelling. Make sure everyone has each word spelled correctly before doing the next word. Keep the lesson fast paced.

1. Take 3 letters and spell **ice**. Do you like to **ice** skate?

2. Add 1 letter and spell **nice**. My cousin is very **nice** to me.

3. Take 4 letters and spell **rent**. We pay the **rent** every month.

4. Change 1 letter and spell **cent**. A penny is worth one **cent**.

5. Use 4 letters again to spell **into**. We walked **into** the library very quietly.

6. Use 4 letters again to spell **torn**. The street in front of my house is all **torn** up.

7. Change 1 letter and spell **corn**. I love **corn** on the cob.

8. Add 2 letters and spell **corner**. The store is on the **corner**.

9. Take 7 letters and spell **concert**. We went to the band **concert**.

10. Use 7 letters again to spell **correct**. Your answer is **correct**.

11. Add your letters to **correct** and you will have the secret word. (Give clues after 1 minute.) The opposite of correct is **incorrect**.

Sort: Display the words on cards in the order they were made and have each word read aloud. Have the related words sorted. Then, have the rhyming words sorted.

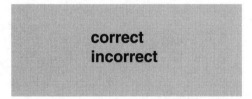

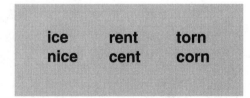

Transfer: Say the following words and have everyone use the rhyming words to spell them:

slice   born   went   twice

Word Wall: Call out five **un** words that can be spelled by using word wall words. Spelling changes may be needed: **unfriendly**, **unhealthy**, **unhappy**, **unwanted**, **unmarried**.

Make Words: Distribute the letters and have everyone write the capitals on the back. After each word is made, show the correct spelling. Make sure everyone has each word spelled correctly before doing the next word. Keep the lesson fast paced.

1. Take 3 letters and spell **ice**. <u>Water freezes to become **ice**.</u>

2. Add 1 letter and spell **nice**. <u>We had a very **nice** day.</u>

3. Change 1 letter and spell **mice**. <u>Cats like to chase **mice**.</u>

4. Use 4 letters again to spell **cent**. <u>I spent all my money and don't have a single **cent**.</u>

5. Change 1 letter and spell **lent**. <u>She **lent** me a pencil.</u>

6. Use 4 letters again to spell **mile**. <u>She lives one **mile** from me.</u>

7. Change 1 letter and spell **pile**. <u>They jumped in the **pile** of leaves.</u>

8. Take 6 letters and spell **pencil**. <u>Can I sharpen my **pencil**?</u>

9. Take 7 letters and spell **compete**. <u>Our team will **compete** in the tournament.</u>

10. Add 1 letter and spell **complete**. <u>You need to **complete** your homework.</u>

11. Add your letters to **complete** and you will have the secret word. (Give clues after 1 minute.)
<u>I was sick and couldn't do all my work, so I got a grade of **incomplete**.</u>

Sort: Display the words on cards in the order they were made and have each word read aloud. Have the related words sorted. Then, have the rhyming words sorted.

| complete | ice cent mile compete |
| incomplete | nice lent pile complete |

Transfer: Say the following words and have everyone use the rhyming words to spell them:

smile spice spent while

Word Wall: Call out five word wall words that are commonly misspelled: **except**, **said**, **with**, **also**, **have**.

Lesson 90

Word Wall Words: immature impossible incorrect incomplete into
Prefixes for Review: in; im

Give everyone a copy of the word wall (p. 162) and/or place the words on the classroom word wall.

Review:

Into is added to the word wall because it is a compound word that is often misspelled. The other words all have the prefix **in** or **im**. The prefix **in** or **im** often turns the root word into an opposite. **Immature** is the opposite of mature. **Incorrect** is the opposite of correct. Have the root words, prefixes, and opposites identified.

immature—**im** mature. The opposite of mature is **immature**.

impossible—**im** possible. The opposite of possible is **impossible**.

incomplete—**in** complete. The opposite of complete is **incomplete**.

incorrect—**in** correct. The opposite of correct is **incorrect**.

Word Wall:

Call out the five words one at a time and have everyone chant the spelling three times for each word. Next, have everyone write the five words as you give sentence clues.

1. He almost won a million dollars but his final answer was _____.

2. If you do not finish your work, you may get a grade of _____.

3. My mother says that my sister does not act her age and is very _____.

4. I am working hard but it is _____ to get this all done in one day.

5. The gate opened and the horses all trotted _____ the ring.

Lesson 91

Letters: a a i i b l n r r
Words: ran ban bran barn nail bail rail rain brain librarian

Make Words: Distribute the letters and have everyone write the capitals on the back. After each word is made, show the correct spelling. Make sure everyone has each word spelled correctly before doing the next word. Keep the lesson fast paced.

1. Take 3 letters and spell **ran**. It started to rain and we **ran** home fast.

2. Change 1 letter and spell **ban**. It is very dry in the woods and there is a **ban** on burning.

3. Add 1 letter and spell **bran**. I like **bran** muffins.

4. Move the letters around and spell **barn**. The horse is in the **barn**.

5. Use 4 letters again to spell **nail**. I am going to **nail** this to the wall.

6. Change 1 letter and spell **bail**. The man had to post **bail** to get out of jail.

7. Change 1 letter and spell **rail**. We tied the horse to the **rail**.

8. Change 1 letter and spell **rain**. It is starting to **rain**.

9. Add 1 letter and spell **brain**. It is amazing all the things your **brain** can do.

10. It's time for the secret word. (Wait 1 minute and then give clues.) The **librarian** helps us choose books in the library.

Sort: Display the words on cards in the order they were made and have each word read aloud. Have the rhyming words sorted.

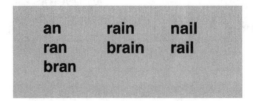

an	rain	nail
ran	brain	rail
bran		

Transfer: Say the following words and have everyone use the rhyming words to spell them:

train trail scan grain

Word Wall: Have everyone look at the word wall and chant and write the five new words: **impossible, immature, into, incorrect, incomplete.**

Lesson 92

Letters: a a i i c g m n s
Words: an can man sing sign main gain again magic magicians

Make Words: Distribute the letters and have everyone write the capitals on the back. After each word is made, show the correct spelling. Make sure everyone has each word spelled correctly before doing the next word. Keep the lesson fast paced.

1. Take 2 letters and spell **an**. Yesterday was **an** awful day!

2. Add 1 letter and spell **can**. I **can** do anything if I really try.

3. Change 1 letter and spell **man**. The **man** was running down the street.

4. Take 4 letters and spell **sing**. Will you **sing** a song for us?

5. Move the letters around and spell **sign**. I am going to get my favorite author to **sign** my book.

6. Use 4 letters again to spell **main**. The **main** reason I am going is because my mom wants me to.

7. Change 1 letter and spell **gain**. If you eat too much, you will **gain** weight.

8. Add 1 letter and spell **again**. I want to watch that movie **again**.

9. Use 5 letters again to spell **magic**. I can do a **magic** trick.

10. Add your letters to **magic** and you will have the secret word. (Give clues after 1 minute.) The **magicians** did a lot of magic tricks.

Sort: Display the words on cards in the order they were made and have each word read aloud. Have the related words sorted. Then, have the rhyming words sorted.

magic
magicians

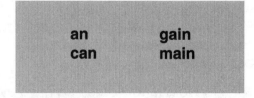

an   gain
can   main

Transfer: Say the following words and have everyone use the rhyming words to spell them:

train brain bran plan

Word Wall: Call out five root words can be spelled by dropping prefixes off word wall words: **complete, mature, correct, possible, appear.**

Lesson 93

Letters: e e e o l m p s y
Words: my spy eyes pole mole seep sleep sleepy employ employees

Make Words: Distribute the letters and have everyone write the capitals on the back. After each word is made, show the correct spelling. Make sure everyone has each word spelled correctly before doing the next word. Keep the lesson fast paced.

1. Take 2 letters and spell **my**. <u>My birthday is in October.</u>

2. Take 3 letters and spell **spy**. <u>The **spy** was arrested and put on trial.</u>

3. Take 4 letters and spell **eyes**. <u>I sleep with my **eyes** closed.</u>

4. Take 4 letters and spell **pole**. <u>The lightning hit the light **pole** and the power went out.</u>

5. Change 1 letter and spell **mole**. <u>A **mole** is a mammal that lives underground.</u>

6. Use 4 letters again to spell **seep**. <u>The water can **seep** through the cracks.</u>

7. Add 1 letter and spell **sleep**. <u>I **sleep** in a bunk bed.</u>

8. Add 1 letter and spell **sleepy**. <u>I am very **sleepy**.</u>

9. Take 6 letters and spell **employ**. <u>The new factory will **employ** hundreds of people.</u>

10. Add your letters to **employ** and you will have the secret word. (Give clues after 1 minute.) <u>People who work for a company or business are called the **employees**.</u>

Sort: Display the words on cards in the order they were made and have each word read aloud. Have the related words sorted. Then, have the rhyming words sorted.

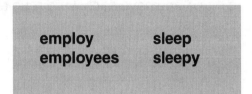

employ   sleep
employees sleepy

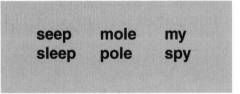

seep   mole   my
sleep pole   spy

Transfer: Say the following words and have everyone use the rhyming words to spell them:

steep beep hole try

Word Wall: Call out five **ly** words that can be spelled using word wall words. Spelling changes may be needed: **completely, correctly, possibly, unexpectedly, happily.**

Lesson 94

Letters: e i i c n s s t t
Words: ice nice test nest sent tent insect nicest iciest tiniest scientist

Make Words: Distribute the letters and have everyone write the capitals on the back. After each word is made, show the correct spelling. Make sure everyone has each word spelled correctly before doing the next word. Keep the lesson fast paced.

1. Take 3 letters and spell **ice**. We put **ice** and drinks in the cooler.

2. Add 1 letter and spell **nice**. It was a very **nice** day.

3. Use 4 letters again to spell **test**. My cousin is a **test** pilot.

4. Change 1 letter and spell **nest**. The mother bird sat on the eggs in her **nest**.

5. Move the letters around and spell **sent**. I **sent** my aunt some flowers for her birthday.

6. Change 1 letter and spell **tent**. The **tent** leaked because it had a hole in it.

7. Take 6 letters and spell **insect**. An ant is an **insect**.

8. Move the letters around and spell **nicest**. This is the **nicest** present I ever got.

9. Use 6 letters to spell **iciest**. It was the coldest, **iciest** day we had all winter.

10. Use 7 letters to spell **tiniest**. We found the **tiniest** baby rabbit in the bushes.

11. It's time for the secret word. (Wait 1 minute and then give clues.) The **scientist** was doing experiments in her laboratory.

Sort: Display the words on cards in the order they were made and have each word read aloud. Have the rhyming words sorted.

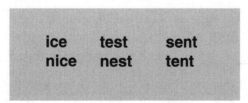

ice	test	sent
nice	nest	tent

Transfer: Say the following words and have everyone use the rhyming words to spell them:

rest chest spent twice

Word Wall: Call out five words meaning "people that do" that end with **er** or **or**: **builder**, **governor**, **sailor**, **winner**, **teacher**.

Lesson 95

Word Wall Words: again employees librarian magicians scientist
Suffixes for Review: ee; ian; ist

Give everyone a copy of the word wall (p. 163) and/or place the words on the classroom word wall.

Review:

Again is added to the word wall because it is often misspelled. The other words all have the suffix **ee, ian**, or **ist**. These suffixes, like **er** and **or**, often indicate a person who does something. Have the root words, suffixes, and spelling changes identified. Have the words used in sentences that show the person/root word connection.

> **employees**—employ **ee** s. The people who are employed are the **employees**.

> **librarian**—library **ian**. The **librarian** works in the library.

> **magicians**—magic **ian** s. **Magicians** do magic tricks.

> **scientist**—science **ist**. A **scientist** does science experiments.

Word Wall:

Call out the five words one at a time and have everyone chant the spelling three times for each word. Next, have everyone write the five words as you give sentence clues.

1. Our _____ knows all the books in the library and helps us pick books we will really like.

2. I like to do experiments and might become a _____ when I grow up.

3. I wish I knew how the _____ do all those magic tricks.

4. When the factory closed, all the _____ lost their jobs.

5. When I see a really good movie, I always want to watch it _____.

Lesson 96

Letters: e i i o n n n s t v
Words: vet vent vest nest sent vote visit tennis invest invent inventions

Make Words: Distribute the letters and have everyone write the capitals on the back. After each word is made, show the correct spelling. Make sure everyone has each word spelled correctly before doing the next word. Keep the lesson fast paced.

1. Take 3 letters and spell **vet**. We took my dog to the **vet**.

2. Add 1 letter and spell **vent**. The heating **vent** was stuck shut.

3. Change 1 letter and spell **vest**. The policeman wore a bulletproof **vest**.

4. Change 1 letter and spell **nest**. Some birds are building a **nest** on our porch.

5. Move the letters around and spell **sent**. Did you get the letter I **sent** you?

6. Use 4 letters again to spell **vote**. Who are you going to **vote** for?

7. Take 5 letters to spell **visit**. We went to **visit** my uncle in the hospital.

8. Take 6 letters and spell **tennis**. Do you like to play **tennis**?

9. Use 6 letters again to spell **invest**. My mom is going to **invest** in some stocks and save them for me to go to college.

10. Change 1 letter and spell **invent**. It is fun to **invent** new things.

11. Add your letters to **invent** and you will have the secret word. (Give clues after 1 minute.) Electric lights and telephones were two of the greatest **inventions**.

Sort: Display the words on cards in the order they were made and have each word read aloud. Have the related words sorted. Then, have the rhyming words sorted.

invent	vent	vest
inventions	sent	nest

Transfer: Say the following words and have everyone use the rhyming words to spell them:

west chest went spent

Word Wall: Have everyone look at the word wall and chant and write the five new words: **again**, **scientist**, **magicians**, **librarian**, **employees**.

Lesson 97

Letters: e i o o c n p r t t
Words: not rot rip trip trot rope ripe ripen rotten protect protection

Make Words: Distribute the letters and have everyone write the capitals on the back. After each word is made, show the correct spelling. Make sure everyone has each word spelled correctly before doing the next word. Keep the lesson fast paced.

1. Take 3 letters and spell **not**. She was sick and did **not** come to school today.
2. Change 1 letter and spell **rot**. If water gets into the wood, it will **rot** it.
3. Take 3 letters and spell **rip**. Sometimes I get mad and **rip** up my paper.
4. Add 1 letter and spell **trip**. We take a **trip** to visit my relatives every summer.
5. Take 4 letters and spell **trot**. I watched the horse **trot** around the track.
6. Use 4 letters again to spell **rope**. At recess we like to jump **rope**.
7. Change 1 letter and spell **ripe**. Next week, the strawberries should be **ripe**.
8. Add 1 letter and spell **ripen**. It takes a long time for strawberries to **ripen**.
9. Take 6 letters and spell **rotten**. I threw away the **rotten** apple.
10. Take 7 letters and spell **protect**. The police officer's job is to **protect** people.
11. Add your letters to **protect** and you will have the secret word. (Give clues after 1 minute.) After the kidnapping, the movie star hired a bodyguard for extra **protection**.

Sort: Display the words on cards in the order they were made and have each word read aloud. Have the related words sorted. Then, have the rhyming words sorted.

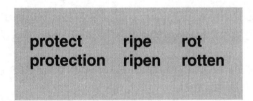

protect	ripe	rot
protection	ripen	rotten

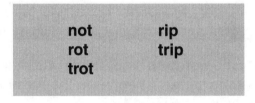

not	rip
rot	trip
trot	

Transfer: Say the following words and have everyone use the rhyming words to spell them:

slip slot ship shot

Word Wall: Call out five root words can be spelled by dropping prefixes off word wall words: **magic, library, employ, science, possible**.

Lesson 98

Letters: a i o o c l n t
Words: at act cat coat taco cool tool action lotion location

Make Words: Distribute the letters and have everyone write the capitals on the back. After each word is made, show the correct spelling. Make sure everyone has each word spelled correctly before doing the next word. Keep the lesson fast paced.

1. Take 2 letters and spell **at**. <u>I saw my friends **at** the game.</u>

2. Add 1 letter and spell **act**. <u>I like to **act** in plays.</u>

3. Move the letters around and spell **cat**. <u>Our **cat** wakes me up every morning.</u>

4. Add 1 letter and spell **coat**. <u>My cat has a thick **coat** of fur.</u>

5. Move the letters around and spell **taco**. <u>I ate a **taco** for lunch.</u>

6. Use 4 letters again to spell **cool**. <u>That was a really **cool** movie.</u>

7. Change 1 letter and spell **tool**. <u>A screwdriver is a handy **tool**.</u>

8. Take 6 letters and spell **action**. <u>I like movies with lots of **action**.</u>

9. Remove the first 2 letters and add 2 more to spell **lotion**. <u>We put suntan **lotion** on before we went to the pool.</u>

10. Add 2 letters to the middle of **lotion** and you will have the secret word. (After 1 minute, give clues.) <u>The director is looking for just the right **location** to film the movie.</u>

Sort: Display the words on cards in the order they were made and have each word read aloud. Have the related words sorted. Then, have the rhyming words sorted.

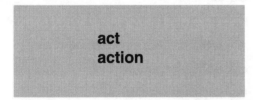

act
action

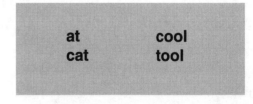

at   cool
cat   tool

Transfer: Say the following words and have everyone use the rhyming words to spell them:

pool flat fool spool

Word Wall: Call out five words that can be spelled by combining root words, prefixes and suffixes from word wall words: **unemployed musicians**, **magical**, **magically**, **completely**.

Make Words: Distribute the letters and have everyone write the capitals on the back. After each word is made, show the correct spelling. Make sure everyone has each word spelled correctly before doing the next word. Keep the lesson fast paced.

1. Take 2 letters and spell **at**. I forgot my homework **at** home.

2. Add 1 letter and spell **act**. My mom says I should **act** my age.

3. Move the letters around and spell **cat**. My **cat** is 15 years old.

4. Add 1 letter and spell **scat**. Sometimes I tell my cat to **scat**.

5. Use 4 letters again to spell **into**. My baby sister gets **into** everything.

6. Use 4 letters again to spell **taco**. Let's go and get a **taco** for lunch.

7. Move the letters around and spell **coat**. Put your **coat** on.

8. Use 4 letters again to spell **oats**. Horses eat **oats**.

9. Add 1 letter and spell **coats**. We all need new winter **coats**.

10. Take 6 letters to spell **action**. Do you like **action** movies?

11. It's time for the secret word. (Wait 1 minute and then give clues.) This year we are going to take two **vacations**.

Sort: Display the words on cards in the order they were made and have each word read aloud. Have the related words sorted. Then, have the rhyming words sorted.

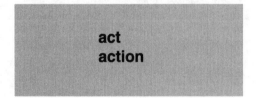

act
action

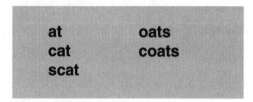

at   oats
cat   coats
scat

Transfer: Say the following words and have everyone use the rhyming words to spell them:

boats goats floats flat

Word Wall: Call out five root words that can be spelled from word wall words: **agree**, **appear**, **ready**, **beauty**, **elevate**.

Lesson 100

Word Wall Words: action inventions location protection vacations
Suffix for Review: tion

Give everyone a copy of the word wall (p. 164) and/or place the words on the classroom word wall.

Review:

All the new word wall words end in **tion**. When **tion** is added to verbs, they often become nouns. Something you **invent** is called an **invention**. Have the root words, suffixes, and spelling changes identified. Have the words used in sentences.

action—act **tion**. The quick **action** of the firemen saved many lives.

inventions—invent **tion** s. The car and the airplane were important **inventions**.

location—locate **tion**. This will be a good **location** for the mall.

protection—protect **tion**. The refugees depended on the U. N. soldiers for **protection**.

vacations—vacate **tion** s. When people go away for **vacations**, their house is usually vacant.

Word Wall: Words

Call out the five words one at a time and have everyone chant the spelling three times for each word. Next, have everyone write the five words as you give sentence clues.

1. We usually go to visit our relatives on our _____.

2. The police officers at the game were there for our _____.

3. I like a movie that has a lot of _____.

4. We walked through the woods looking for a good _____ to pitch our tents.

5. The television and the VCR were wonderful _____.

Lessons 101-105
Suffix: sion

Lesson 101

Letters: i i o u c d n s s s
Words: do on Don nod undo suds cuds cousin discuss discussion

Make Words: Distribute the letters and have everyone write the capitals on the back. After each word is made, show the correct spelling. Make sure everyone has each word spelled correctly before doing the next word. Keep the lesson fast paced.

1. Take 2 letters and spell **do**. What **do** you want to eat?

2. Take 2 letters and spell **on**. We went to New York **on** the train.

3. Add 1 letter and spell **Don**. My best friend's name is **Don**.

4. Move the letters around and spell **nod**. **Nod** your head if you agree.

5. Take 4 letters and spell **undo**. Can you help me **undo** the knot in this string?

6. Take 4 letters and spell **suds**. We filled the tub with water and soap and made a lot of **suds**.

7. Change 1 letter and spell **cuds**. Cows chew their **cuds**.

8. Take 6 letters and spell **cousin**. My **cousin** is staying with me for the summer.

9. Take 7 letters and spell **discuss**. The teacher put us in groups and told us to **discuss** the events of the story.

10. Add your letters to **discuss** and you will have the secret word. (Give clues after 1 minute.) Our group had a very good **discussion**.

Sort: Display the words on cards in the order they were made and have each word read aloud. Have the related words sorted. Then, have the rhyming words sorted.

discuss	do
discussion	undo

cuds	on
suds	Don

Transfer: Say the following words and have everyone use the rhyming words to spell them:

con buds thuds Ron

Word Wall: Have everyone look at the word wall and chant and write the five new words: **inventions, location, protection, action, vacations**.

Lesson 102

Letters: e i o o l n p s x
Words: pool loop soon spoon snoop noose loose loosen ponies explosion

Make Words: Distribute the letters and have everyone write the capitals on the back. After each word is made, show the correct spelling. Make sure everyone has each word spelled correctly before doing the next word. Keep the lesson fast paced.

1. Take 4 letters and spell **pool**. We filled the **pool** with water.
2. Move the letters around and spell **loop**. **Loop** this rope around the pole.
3. Use 4 letters again to spell **soon**. I will be home **soon**.
4. Add 1 letter and spell **spoon**. I need a **spoon** to eat my soup.
5. Move the letters around and spell **snoop**. I am not supposed to **snoop** in my sister's room.
6. Use 5 letters again to spell **noose**. He tied a **noose** in the end of the rope.
7. Change 1 letter and spell **loose**. I have a **loose** tooth that is going to fall out.
8. Add 1 letter and spell **loosen**. I wiggle my tooth to try to **loosen** it.
9. Use 6 letters to spell **ponies**. We rode the **ponies** at the fair.
10. It's time for the secret word. (Wait 1 minute and then give clues.) There was a big **explosion** when the fireworks started.

Sort: Display the words on cards in the order they were made and have each word read aloud. Have the related words sorted. Then, have the rhyming words sorted.

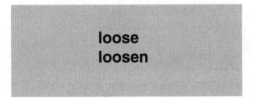

loose
loosen

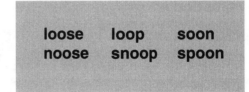

loose   loop   soon
noose   snoop   spoon

Transfer: Say the following words and have everyone use the rhyming words to spell them:

moon goose scoop troop

Word Wall: Call out five root words that can be spelled by dropping prefixes off word wall words: **act**, **locate**, **protect**, **vacate**, **invent**.

Lesson 103

Letters: i o o u c f n n s
Words: in fin fun sun son soon noon onion union cousin confusion

Make Words: Distribute the letters and have everyone write the capitals on the back. After each word is made, show the correct spelling. Make sure everyone has each word spelled correctly before doing the next word. Keep the lesson fast paced.

1. Take 2 letters and spell **in**. We are **in** school during the day.

2. Add 1 letter and spell **fin**. I saw the **fin** of the dolphin come out of the water.

3. Change 1 letter and spell **fun**. It is **fun** to watch dolphins swim and play.

4. Change 1 letter and spell **sun**. We get solar energy from the **sun**.

5. Change 1 letter and spell a different word **son**. The man and his **son** went fishing.

6. Add 1 letter and spell **soon**. My birthday is coming **soon**.

7. Change 1 letter and spell **noon**. We will eat at **noon**.

8. Use 5 letters to spell **onion**. She cried when she peeled the **onion**.

9. Change 1 letter and spell **union**. The workers all belong to the **union**.

10. Take 6 letters and spell **cousin**. My **cousin** is 12 years old.

11. It's time for the secret word. (Wait 1 minute and then give clues.) There was a lot of **confusion** when the power went off and the whole room went dark.

Sort: Display the words on cards in the order they were made and have each word read aloud. Have the rhyming words sorted.

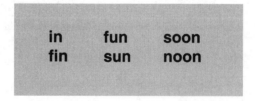

in	fun	soon
fin	sun	noon

Transfer: Say the following words and have everyone use the rhyming words to spell them:

spoon spin spun twin

Word Wall: Call out five words that can be spelled by combining root words, prefixes, and suffixes from word wall words: **inventor**, **unprotected**, **located**, **actor**, **reinvented**.

Lesson 104

Letters: e i i o c d n s
Words: in ice one once done nice side inside second decision

Make Words: Distribute the letters and have everyone write the capitals on the back. After each word is made, show the correct spelling. Make sure everyone has each word spelled correctly before doing the next word. Keep the lesson fast paced.

1. Take 2 letters and spell **in**. <u>What grade are you **in**?</u>
2. Take 3 letters and spell **ice**. <u>What flavor of **ice** cream do you like best?</u>
3. Take 3 letters and spell **one**. <u>Chocolate chip is my favorite **one**.</u>
4. Add 1 letter and spell **once**. <u>**Once** upon a time there were three pigs.</u>
5. Use 4 letters again to spell **done**. <u>Is your homework **done**?</u>
6. Use 4 letters again to spell **nice**. <u>**Nice** job!</u>
7. Use 4 letters again to spell **side**. <u>We sat on the right **side**.</u>
8. Add 2 letters and you can spell **inside**. <u>We went **inside** when it began to rain.</u>
9. Use 6 letters to spell **second**. <u>My brother is in the **second** grade.</u>
10. It's time for the secret word. (Wait 1 minute and then give clues.) <u>Choosing which team to cheer for is a hard **decision** because I like both teams.</u>

Sort: Display the words on cards in the order they were made and have each word read aloud. Have the related words sorted. Then, have the rhyming words sorted.

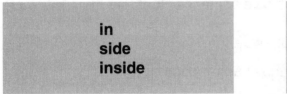

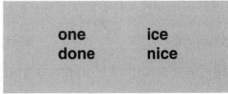

Transfer: Say the following words and have everyone use the rhyming words to spell them:

twice slice none mice

Word Wall: Call out the five contractions and have everyone chant and write them: **don't, they're, doesn't, wouldn't, shouldn't**.

Lesson 105

Word Wall Words: confusion cousin decision discussion explosion
Suffix for Review: sion

Give everyone a copy of the word wall (p. 165) and/or place the words on the classroom word wall.

Review:

Cousin is added to the word wall because it is a commonly misspelled word. The other word wall words end in **sion.** When **sion** is added to verbs, they often become nouns. When you **discuss** something, you are having a **discussion.** Have the root words, suffixes, and spelling changes identified. Notice that for words that end in **de**, the **d** and **e** are dropped and **sion** is added. Have the words used in sentences.

confusion—confuse **sion**. We read the directions but there was still a lot of **confusion** about what we were supposed to do.

decision—decide **sion**. After listening to all the evidence, the judge made a **decision**.

discussion—discuss **sion**. Our group had a very good **discussion**.

explosion—explode **sion**. The dynamite was set off and there was a huge **explosion**.

Word Wall:

Call out the five words one at a time and have everyone chant the spelling three times for each word. Next, have everyone write the five words as you give sentence clues.

1. You could hear the _____ a mile away.

2. The jury sent a message to the judge that they had reached a _____.

3. We got in groups and had a good _____ about the story.

4. When the tornado struck, people ran around in _____.

5. I like to play video games with my _____.

Lesson 106

Letters: a a e b h l s w
Words: law saw was wash able heal seal sale whale washable

Make Words: Distribute the letters and have everyone write the capitals on the back. After each word is made, show the correct spelling. Make sure everyone has each word spelled correctly before doing the next word. Keep the lesson fast paced.

1. Take 3 letters and spell **law**. <u>We have a leash **law** for dogs in our town.</u>
2. Change 1 letter and spell **saw**. <u>I **saw** a good movie last night.</u>
3. Move the letters around and spell **was**. <u>The movie **was** about space travel.</u>
4. Add 1 letter and spell **wash**. <u>We **wash** our dishes in the dishwasher.</u>
5. Take 4 letters and spell **able**. <u>My grandpa is blind but he is still **able** to do a lot of things.</u>
6. Use 4 letters again to spell **heal**. <u>I broke my arm but it is beginning to **heal**.</u>
7. Change 1 letter and spell **seal**. <u>There was a baby **seal** at the aquarium.</u>
8. Move the letters around and spell **sale**. <u>I like to buy things on **sale** and save money.</u>
9. Remove the **s** and add 2 letters to spell **whale**. <u>A **whale** is a huge animal.</u>
10. Add your letters to a word we already made and you will have the secret word. (Give clues after 1 minute.) <u>I don't like to go the cleaners so I try to buy only clothes that are **washable**.</u>

Sort: Display the words on cards in the order they were made and have each word read aloud. Have the related words sorted. Then, have the rhyming words sorted.

wash
washable

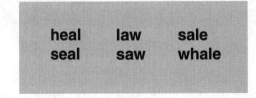

heal   law   sale
seal   saw   whale

Transfer: Say the following words and have everyone use the rhyming words to spell them:

claw stale steal thaw

Word Wall: Have everyone look at the word wall and chant and write the five new words: **cousin**, **explosion**, **discussion**, **decision**, **confusion**.

Lesson 107

Letters: a e e e b d d l n p
Words: and land band able deed need needed needle landed depend dependable

Make Words: Distribute the letters and have everyone write the capitals on the back. After each word is made, show the correct spelling. Make sure everyone has each word spelled correctly before doing the next word. Keep the lesson fast paced.

1. Take 3 letters and spell **and**. I like cookies **and** milk.

2. Add 1 letter and spell **land**. The airplane should **land** at 10:30.

3. Change 1 letter and spell **band**. I would like to play the drums in the **band**.

4. Take 4 letters and spell **able**. I think I would be **able** to be a great drummer.

5. Use 4 letters again to spell **deed**. Girl scouts and boy scouts are always trying to do a good **deed**.

6. Change 1 letter and spell **need**. What do you **need**?

7. Add 2 letters and you can spell **needed**. The refugees **needed** a place to live.

8. Remove the **ed** and add 2 letters and spell **needle**. I need my glasses to thread a **needle**.

9. Take 6 letters to spell **landed**. The airplane **landed** right on time.

10. Use 6 letters to spell **depend**. I can **depend** on my friends to help me when I need help.

11. Add your letters to **depend** and you will have the secret word. (Give clues after 1 minute.) My friends are very **dependable**.

Sort: Display the words on cards in the order they were made and have each word read aloud. Have the related words sorted. Then, have the rhyming words sorted.

depend	need	land
dependable	needed	landed

land	deed
band	need
and	

Transfer: Say the following words and have everyone use the rhyming words to spell them:

> brand breed speed grand

Word Wall: Call out five root words can be spelled by dropping prefixes off word wall words: **discuss, decide, explode, confuse, locate.**

Lesson 108

Letters: e e i b l r r t
Words: it tie lie lit let bet bit bite relit retire terrible

Make Words: Distribute the letters and have everyone write the capitals on the back. After each word is made, show the correct spelling. Make sure everyone has each word spelled correctly before doing the next word. Keep the lesson fast paced.

1. Take 2 letters and spell **it**. <u>**It** is going to be a great day.</u>
2. Take 3 letters and spell **tie**. <u>I am teaching my brother how to **tie** his shoes.</u>
3. Change 1 letter and spell **lie**. <u>It is wrong to tell a **lie**.</u>
4. Change 1 letter and spell **lit**. <u>We **lit** a fire in the fireplace.</u>
5. Change 1 letter and spell **let**. <u>I hope your mom will **let** you come over and play.</u>
6. Change 1 letter and spell **bet**. <u>I **bet** she will.</u>
7. Change 1 letter and spell **bit**. <u>I got **bit** by a mosquito.</u>
8. Add 1 letter and spell **bite**. <u>A mosquito **bite** is very itchy.</u>
9. Use 5 letters to spell **relit**. <u>The fire went out so we **relit** it.</u>
10. Use 6 letters to spell **retire**. <u>My uncle is going to **retire** from his job next year.</u>
11. It's time for the secret word. (Wait 1 minute and then give clues.) <u>I had a **terrible**, horrible, no-good, very bad day!</u>

Sort: Display the words on cards in the order they were made and have each word read aloud. Have the related words sorted. Then, have the rhyming words sorted.

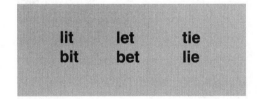

lit
relit

lit   let   tie
bit   bet   lie

Transfer: Say the following words and have everyone use the rhyming words to spell them:

pie die pet pit

Word Wall: Call out five words that can be spelled by combining root words, prefixes, and suffixes from word wall words: **confusing, decided, exploding, improbable, unreal.**

Letters: e e i b l n s s
Words: see bee Ben Bess less lens sense lenses lessen sensible

Make Words: Distribute the letters and have everyone write the capitals on the back. After each word is made, show the correct spelling. Make sure everyone has each word spelled correctly before doing the next word. Keep the lesson fast paced.

1. Take 3 letters and spell **see**. <u>What animals did you **see** at the zoo?</u>

2. Change 1 letter and spell **bee**. <u>I got stung by a **bee**.</u>

3. Change 1 letter and spell **Ben**. <u>**Ben** got stung by a wasp.</u>

4. Take 4 letters and spell **Bess**. <u>**Bess** got stung by a hornet.</u>

5. Change 1 letter and spell **less**. <u>Five is **less** than seven.</u>

6. Change 1 letter and spell **lens**. <u>Her contact **lens** fell out.</u>

7. Take 5 letters to spell **sense**. <u>Sometimes math just doesn't make **sense** to me.</u>

8. Take 6 letters and spell **lenses**. <u>She got new contact **lenses**.</u>

9. Move the letters around and spell **lessen**. <u>Eating too much before a race will **lessen** your chances of winning.</u>

10. It's time for the secret word. Drop the **e** and add your letters to a word we already made and you will have it. (Wait 1 minute and then give clues.) <u>That was a very **sensible** answer.</u>

Sort: Display the words on cards in the order they were made and have each word read aloud. Have the related words sorted. Then, have the rhyming words sorted.

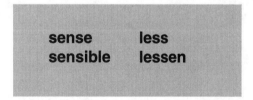

sense	less
sensible	lessen

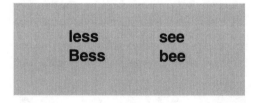

less	see
Bess	bee

Transfer: Say the following words and have everyone use the rhyming words to spell them:

mess chess bless free

Word Wall: Call out the five commonly misspelled words and have everyone chant and write them: **cousin**, **again**, **their** (their cousin), **there** (over there), **they're** (they are).

Lesson 110

Word Wall Words: dependable sensible terrible was washable
Suffixes for Review: able; ible

Give everyone a copy of the word wall (p. 166) and/or place the words on the classroom word wall.

Review:

Was is added to the word wall because it is a commonly misspelled word. The other word wall words end in **able** or **ible.** Have the root words, suffixes, and spelling changes identified. Have the words used in sentences.

dependable—depend **able**. <u>Someone you can depend on is **dependable**.</u>

washable—wash **able**. <u>Something that you can wash is **washable**.</u>

sensible—sense **ible**. <u>Something that makes sense is **sensible**.</u>

terrible—terror **ible**. <u>Something that makes you feel terror is **terrible**.</u>

Word Wall:

Call out the five words one at a time and have everyone chant the spelling three times for each word. Next, have everyone write the five words as you give sentence clues.

1. My mom always gives me very good and _____ advice.

2. I always buy clothes that are _____ and don't need ironing.

3. The day our house was struck by a tornado was a _____ day.

4. My friend and I do the paper route and he is always there and is very _____.

5. The only time he _____ not there was when he broke his foot.

Lessons 111-115
Suffix: ment

Lesson 111

Letters: e e o j m n n t y
Words: net yet jet joy toy one none money enemy enjoy enjoyment

Make Words: Distribute the letters and have everyone write the capitals on the back. After each word is made, show the correct spelling. Make sure everyone has each word spelled correctly before doing the next word. Keep the lesson fast paced.

1. Take 3 letters and spell **net**. <u>He shot the ball right into the **net**.</u>

2. Change 1 letter and spell **yet**. <u>Dinner is not quite ready **yet**.</u>

3. Change 1 letter and spell **jet**. <u>The **jet** plane flew really fast.</u>

4. Take 3 letters and spell **joy**. <u>It was a **joy** to see how happy they were.</u>

5. Change 1 letter and spell **toy**. <u>A **toy** is something to play with.</u>

6. Take 3 letters and spell **one**. <u>Our team was number **one** this year.</u>

7. Add 1 letter and spell **none**. <u>**None** of the other teams came close to beating us.</u>

8. Take 5 letters to spell **money**. <u>It costs a lot of **money** to go to college.</u>

9. Use 5 letters again to spell **enemy**. <u>The marines landed in **enemy** territory.</u>

10. Use 5 letters again to spell **enjoy**. <u>I have seen this movie and you will really **enjoy** it.</u>

11. Add your letters to **enjoy** and you will have the secret word. (Give clues after 1 minute.)
   <u>We got a lot of **enjoyment** out of the trips we took every summer.</u>

Sort: Display the words on cards in the order they were made and have each word read aloud. Have the related words sorted. Then, have the rhyming words sorted.

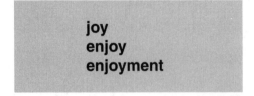

joy
enjoy
enjoyment

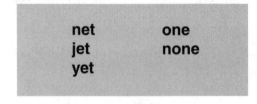

net	one
jet	none
yet	

Transfer: Say the following words and have everyone use the rhyming words to spell them:

done bet get wet

Word Wall: Have everyone look at the word wall and chant and write the five new words: **dependable, washable, was, sensible, terrible.**

Lesson 112

Make Words: Distribute the letters and have everyone write the capitals on the back. After each word is made, show the correct spelling. Make sure everyone has each word spelled correctly before doing the next word. Keep the lesson fast paced.

1. Take 3 letters and spell **eat**. I like to **eat** spaghetti and meatballs.

2. Add 1 letter and spell **neat**. I keep my room very **neat**.

3. Change 1 letter and spell **meat**. Vegetarians do not eat any **meat**.

4. Change 1 letter and spell **mean**. Sometimes kids can be very **mean**.

5. Move the letters around and spell **name**. My **name** is Pat.

6. Change 1 letter and spell **tame**. Is that rabbit **tame**?

7. Take 5 letters to spell **treat**. We will have a special **treat** on Friday afternoon.

8. Use 5 letters again to spell **eaten**. Someone has **eaten** all the cookies!

9. Take 6 letters and spell **meaner**. My neighbor is mean but his big brother is even **meaner**.

10. Move the letters around and spell **rename**. Our community is going to **rename** our school after a local basketball star.

11. Add your letters to a word we already made and you will have the secret word. (Give clues after 1 minute.) The cat was scared and had obviously suffered from very bad **treatment**.

Sort: Display the words on cards in the order they were made and have each word read aloud. Have the related words sorted. Then, have the rhyming words sorted.

treat	name	mean	eat
treatment	rename	meaner	eaten

eat	name
neat	tame
meat	
treat	

Transfer: Say the following words and have everyone use the rhyming words to spell them:

fame flame cheat blame

Word Wall: Call out five root words that can be spelled by dropping prefixes off word wall words: **depend, wash, sense, explode, decide.**

Lesson 113

Letters: e e e i c m n t t x
Words: ice nice mice tent cent next exit excite extinct excitement

Make Words: Distribute the letters and have everyone write the capitals on the back. After each word is made, show the correct spelling. Make sure everyone has each word spelled correctly before doing the next word. Keep the lesson fast paced.

1. Take 3 letters and spell **ice**. The water in the pond had frozen to **ice**.

2. Add 1 letter and spell **nice**. We had a very **nice** time at the party.

3. Change 1 letter and spell **mice**. My friend has six pet **mice**.

4. Take 4 letters and spell **tent**. We sleep in the **tent** in the backyard.

5. Change 1 letter and spell **cent**. A penny is worth one **cent**.

6. Use 4 letters again to spell **next**. It is our turn **next**.

7. Take 4 letters and spell **exit**. The **exit** is the way to go out.

8. Take 6 letters and spell **excite**. Be careful not to **excite** the baby too much.

9. Take 7 letters and spell **extinct**. Dinosaurs are **extinct**.

10. Add your letters to a word we already made and you will have the secret word. (Give clues after 1 minute.) There was a lot of **excitement** in the crowd when the home team was about to win the game.

Sort: Display the words on cards in the order they were made and have each word read aloud. Have the related words sorted. Then, have the rhyming words sorted.

excite
excitement

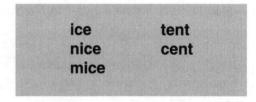

ice	tent
nice	cent
mice	

Transfer: Say the following words and have everyone use the rhyming words to spell them:

dice price rice twice

Word Wall: Call out five words that can be spelled by combining root words, prefixes, and suffixes from word wall words: **unbeatable**, **disagreeable**, **carelessly**, **helpfully**, **reappeared**.

Lesson 114

Letters: e e i m n n s t t v
Words: test vest nest sent vent event tennis invent invest investment

Make Words: Distribute the letters and have everyone write the capitals on the back. After each word is made, show the correct spelling. Make sure everyone has each word spelled correctly before doing the next word. Keep the lesson fast paced.

1. Take 4 letters and spell **test**. How did you do on the **test**?
2. Change 1 letter and spell **vest**. The suit had pants, a jacket, and a **vest**.
3. Change 1 letter and spell **nest**. The birds are building a **nest**.
4. Move the letters around and spell **sent**. I **sent** my cousin an e-mail.
5. Change 1 letter and spell **vent**. Our dog likes to sleep next to the heating **vent**.
6. Add 1 letter and spell **event**. The Thanksgiving football game was an annual **event**.
7. Take 6 letters and spell **tennis**. Have you ever played **tennis**?
8. Take 6 letters and spell **invent**. I would like to **invent** a time travel machine.
9. Change 1 letter and spell **invest**. We are going to **invest** in some bonds and save them for college.
10. Add your letters to **invest** and you will have the secret word. (Give clues after 1 minute.) The stocks and bonds were a very good **investment**.

Sort: Display the words on cards in the order they were made and have each word read aloud. Have the related words sorted. Then, have the rhyming words sorted.

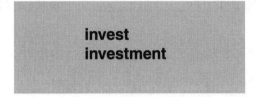

invest
investment

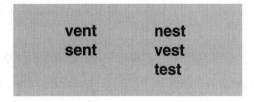

vent   nest
sent   vest
        test

Transfer: Say the following words and have everyone use the rhyming words to spell them:

bent went west pest

Word Wall: Call out the five commonly misspelled words and have everyone chant and write them: **cousin, again, was, want, went.**

Lesson 115

Word Wall Words: enjoyment excitement investment none treatment
Suffix for Review: ment

Give everyone a copy of the word wall (p. 167) and/or place the words on the classroom word wall.

Review:

None is added to the word wall because it is a commonly misspelled word. The other word wall words end in **ment.** Have the root words and suffixes identified. Have the words used in sentences.

enjoyment—enjoy **ment**. My parents get **enjoyment** from watching old movies.

excitement—excite **ment**. There was a lot of **excitement** about the fall festival.

investment—invest **ment**. My dad says **investment** in new schools is a good use of our money.

treatment—treat **ment**. Scientist have invented a new **treatment** for cancer.

Word Wall:

Call out the five words one at a time and have everyone chant the spelling three times for each word. Next, have everyone write the five words as you give sentence clues.

1. I went to the store to buy a new video but when I got there they had _____ left.

2. My mom says stocks and bonds are the best _____.

3. My uncle is in the hospital and he is getting excellent _____ for his medical problems.

4. We visit people in nursing homes and they get a lot of _____ out of our visits.

5. There was a lot of _____ in our town as we prepared for the parade.

Lesson 116

Letters: i o o o u n p s s
Words: on in pin nip snip spin soon spoon poison poisonous

Make Words: Distribute the letters and have everyone write the capitals on the back. After each word is made, show the correct spelling. Make sure everyone has each word spelled correctly before doing the next word. Keep the lesson fast paced.

1. Take 2 letters and spell **on**. <u>Put the book **on** the table.</u>

2. Change 1 letter and spell **in**. <u>On rainy days, we play **in** the house.</u>

3. Add 1 letter and spell **pin**. <u>The teacher wore a pretty butterfly **pin**.</u>

4. Move the letters around and spell **nip**. <u>My puppy likes to run after me and **nip** at my feet.</u>

5. Add 1 letter and spell **snip**. <u>My baby sister took my scissors and tried to **snip** off her hair.</u>

6. Move the letters around and spell **spin**. <u>I like to **spin** around until I get dizzy.</u>

7. Take 4 letters and spell **soon**. <u>We will be there **soon**.</u>

8. Add 1 letter and spell **spoon**. <u>I need a **spoon** to eat this ice cream.</u>

9. Use 6 letters to spell **poison**. <u>Have you ever had **poison** ivy?</u>

10. Add your letters to **poison** and you will have the secret word. (Give clues after 1 minute.)
    <u>I am scared of snakes even though I know that most snakes are not **poisonous**.</u>

Sort: Display the words on cards in the order they were made and have each word read aloud. Have the related words sorted. Then, have the rhyming words sorted.

poison		
poisonous		

in	nip	soon
pin	snip	spoon
spin		

Transfer: Say the following words and have everyone use the rhyming words to spell them:

chip ship chin noon

Word Wall: Have everyone look at the word wall and chant and write the five new words: **enjoyment, treatment, investment, excitement, none.**

Lesson 117

Letters: a e o u d g n r s
Words: our use used sour sound round ground around garden danger dangerous

Make Words: Distribute the letters and have everyone write the capitals on the back. After each word is made, show the correct spelling. Make sure everyone has each word spelled correctly before doing the next word. Keep the lesson fast paced.

1. Take 3 letters and spell **our**. <u>**Our** class is the smartest class in the school.</u>
2. Take 3 letters and spell **use**. <u>We **use** the computers to publish our writing.</u>
3. Add 1 letter and spell **used**. <u>My dad bought a **used** truck.</u>
4. Take 4 letters and spell **sour**. <u>I like milk but not when it is old and **sour**.</u>
5. Remove the r and add 2 letters to spell **sound**. <u>I love the **sound** of the waves in the ocean.</u>
6. Change 1 letter and spell **round**. <u>A beach ball is **round**.</u>
7. Add 1 letter and spell **ground**. <u>I dropped my ice cream cone on the **ground**.</u>
8. Change 1 letter and spell **around**. <u>We all ran **around** the circle.</u>
9. Use 6 letters to spell **garden**. <u>We grow tomatoes and cucumbers in the **garden**.</u>
10. Move the letters around and spell **danger**. <u>The mountain climbers, who became stranded in the blizzard, were in great **danger**.</u>
11. Add your letters to **danger** and you will have the secret word. (Give clues after 1 minute.) <u>Mountain climbing can be very **dangerous**.</u>

Sort: Display the words on cards in the order they were made and have each word read aloud. Have the related words sorted. Then, have the rhyming words sorted.

danger	round	use
dangerous	around	used

round	our
ground	sour
around	
sound	

Transfer: Say the following words and have everyone use the rhyming words to spell them:

found pound mound bound

Word Wall: Call out five root words that can be spelled by dropping prefixes off word wall words: **enjoy, invest, excite, invest, confuse.**

Make Words: Distribute the letters and have everyone write the capitals on the back. After each word is made, show the correct spelling. Make sure everyone has each word spelled correctly before doing the next word. Keep the lesson fast paced.

1. Take 3 letters and spell **tie**. <u>**Tie** your shoes, please.</u>
2. Change 1 letter and spell **lie**. <u>My friend got in trouble for telling a **lie**.</u>
3. Take 3 letters and spell **eat**. <u>We will **eat** at 6:00.</u>
4. Add 1 letter and spell **heat**. <u>My grandma always turns the **heat** up.</u>
5. Take 4 letters and spell **each**. <u>She brought three books for **each** of us.</u>
6. Add 1 letter and spell **teach**. <u>Sometimes I **teach** my little brother how to do things.</u>
7. Move the letters around and spell **cheat**. <u>I don't like to play with people who **cheat**.</u>
8. Use 5 letters again to spell **title**. <u>What is the **title** of the book you are reading?</u>
9. Use 6 letters to spell **cattle**. <u>My uncle lives out west and raises **cattle**.</u>
10. It's time for the secret word. (Wait 1 minute and then give clues.) <u>I like to play all kinds of sports and people say I am very **athletic**.</u>

Sort: Display the words on cards in the order they were made and have each word read aloud. Have the rhyming words sorted.

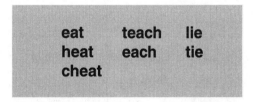

eat	teach	lie
heat	each	tie
cheat		

Transfer: Say the following words and have everyone use the rhyming words to spell them:

peach   reach   seat   treat

Word Wall: Call out five words that can be spelled by combining root words, prefixes, and suffixes from word wall words: **disagreement**, **unemployment**, **government**, **unhappier**, **remarried**.

Lesson 119

Letters: a a i c f n s t t
Words: an can fan fat cat act fact fast cast fantastic

Make Words: Distribute the letters and have everyone write the capitals on the back. After each word is made, show the correct spelling. Make sure everyone has each word spelled correctly before doing the next word. Keep the lesson fast paced.

1. Take 2 letters and spell **an**. When I grow up, I want to be **an** actor.

2. Add 1 letter and spell **can**. I am heating this **can** of soup for lunch.

3. Change 1 letter and spell **fan**. The **fan** helps to cool us off.

4. Change 1 letter and spell **fat**. My dog does not get enough exercise and he is getting **fat**.

5. Change 1 letter and spell **cat**. My **cat** is getting fat, too.

6. Move the letters around and spell **act**. I love to **act** in plays.

7. Add 1 letter and spell **fact**. In **fact**, I am a very good actor.

8. Change 1 letter and spell **fast**. My students are very **fast** learners.

9. Change 1 letter and spell **cast**. I once broke my arm and had to wear a **cast** for two months.

10. It's time for the secret word. (Wait 1 minute and then give clues.) You have done a **fantastic** job of making words and figuring out the secret words.

Sort: Display the words on cards in the order they were made and have each word read aloud. Have the rhyming words sorted.

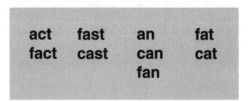

act	fast	an	fat
fact	cast	can	cat
		fan	

Transfer: Say the following words and have everyone use the rhyming words to spell them:

last blast than flat

Word Wall: Call out the five commonly misspelled words and have everyone chant and write them: **cousin**, **again**, **was**, **none**, **also**.

Lesson 120

Word Wall Words: around athletic dangerous fantastic poisonous
Suffixes for Review: ous; ic

Give everyone a copy of the word wall (p. 168) and/or place the words on the classroom word wall.

Review:

Around is added to the word wall because it is a commonly misspelled word. The other word wall words end in **ous** or **ic.** Have the root words, suffixes, and spelling changes identified. Have the words used in sentences.

athletic—athlete **ic**. Someone who is a good athlete is **athletic**.

fantastic—fantasy **ic**. Something that is wonderful and hard to believe is **fantastic**.

dangerous—danger **ous**. The soldiers set out on a **dangerous** mission.

poisonous—poison **ous**. Be careful around some plants because they are **poisonous**.

Word Wall:

Call out the five words one at a time and have everyone chant the spelling three times for each word. Next, have everyone write the five words as you give sentence clues.

1. Being outside in a thunderstorm is very _____.

2. Most mushrooms are good to eat but some wild mushrooms are _____.

3. My brother plays baseball, tennis, and basketball and is very _____.

4. That was the most _____ movie I ever saw!

5. Let's walk all _____ the park.

Prefixes and Suffixes
Review Activities

These review activities can be done when all the lessons are completed or whenever you feel the need and have the time to review important concepts. The examples include all 120 word wall words. If you use these activities before you have all the words on the word wall, adjust the activity for the words currently on the wall. Review by calling out words and having students chant and write them, by giving sentence clues to words and having students decide which word fits in the sentence, or by playing WORDO or Be a Mind Reader.

Review Suffixes and Spelling Changes

The word Wall contains these example words for the most common suffixes.

s/es	addresses computers countries crashes employees governors inventions lunches magicians monkeys vacations winners
ed	floated fried grabbed married recalled refilled squirted wanted unexpected used
ing	stopping swimming watching writing
en	broken frighten hidden unbeaten written
y	healthy rainy
al	musical national
er/est	faster funnier heavier thinner biggest easiest hardest smallest
er/or	computers skater teacher winners builder editor elevator governors sailor
ian/ist/ee	librarian magicians employees scientist
ly	brightly friendly probably really
ful/less	beautiful careful helpless weightless
ness	darkness happiness readiness sadness
tion/sion	action inventions location protection vacations confusion discussion decision explosion
able/ible	dependable washable sensible terrible
ment	enjoyment excitement investment treatment
ous	dangerous poisonous
ic	athletic fantastic

Review Prefixes

re (**back** or **again**)   rebuild refilled replace recalled
un (**not** or **opposite**)   unbeaten unexpected
dis (**not** or **opposite**)   disagree disappear
in/im (**not** or **opposite**)   immature impossible incorrect incomplete

Review Compounds and Contractions

anybody anywhere everyone something don't doesn't shouldn't wouldn't they're

Review Commonly Misspelled Words

again also any (anybody) are around country cousin every (everyone) except friend (friendly) have into none our right said some (something) their there they was want (wanted) went were what where (anywhere) with write (writing)

Extension Activities

The word wall words can help students spell many other words. Some of these words rhyme with the word wall word or with the root word. Other words can be spelled by combining prefixes, suffixes, and root words. To help students learn how the word wall words they can spell can help them spell lots of other words, call out some words and have students tell you which word will help them spell them. Then, have them chant and write the extension words. Students also enjoy playing WORDO with the extension words.

Rhyming Words

Students should be able to spell these rhyming words based on word wall words. When they become more adept with prefixes, suffixes, and spelling changes, call out these rhyming words with added prefixes and suffixes.

act fact pact tact

action faction fraction traction

round bound found ground hound mound pound sound wound

big dig fig gig jig pig rig twig wig

bright blight fight flight fright knight light might night plight right sight slight tight

broke choke Coke® joke poke smoke spoke stoke stroke woke

broken spoken token woken

care bare blare dare fare flare glare mare rare scare share snare spare square stare

crash ash bash brash cash clash dash flash gash hash lash mash rash sash slash smash splash stash thrash trash

dark bark lark mark park shark spark stark

fast blast cast last mast past vast

float bloat boat coat gloat goat moat oat throat

fry by cry dry fly my pry shy sky sly spry spy sty why

fried cried died dried pried shied tied tried

fun bun gun nun pun run shun spun stun sun

grab blab cab crab dab drab flab gab jab lab nab scab stab tab

happy pappy sappy scrappy snappy

hard card lard yard

hide bride glide pride ride side slide snide stride tide wide

lunch brunch bunch crunch hunch munch punch scrunch

rain brain chain drain gain grain main pain plain slain Spain sprain stain strain train

real deal heal meal seal squeal steal teal veal zeal

call all ball fall gall hall mall small squall stall tall wall

fill bill chill dill drill fill frill gill grill hill ill kill mill pill shrill sill skill spill still thrill till will

place ace brace face grace lace pace place race space trace

sad ad bad dad fad grad had lad mad pad tad

sail ail bail fail frail hail jail mail nail pail quail rail sail snail tail train wail

skate ate crate date fate gate grate hate late mate plate rate slate

squirt dirt flirt shirt skirt

stop bop chop cop crop drop flop hop mop plop pop prop shop slop top

swim brim dim grim him prim rim skim slim trim whim

teach beach bleach each peach reach

thin bin chin fin grin in kin pin shin sin skin spin tin twin win

treat beat bleat cheat eat feat heat meat neat pleat seat wheat

went bent cent dent lent rent scent sent spent tent vent

write bite cite kite quite rite site spite sprite white

Root Words

These words can be spelled by combining a root word from the word wall with the prefixes and suffixes taught.

act action acts acted acting actor actors react reacts reactor reactors reaction reactions

address addresses addressed addressing

agree disagree agrees agreed agreeing agreement agreements agreeable disagreement disagreements disagreeable

appear disappear appeared appearing appears disappears disappeared disappearing reappear reappears reappeared reappearing

athlete athletes athletic

beat beats beating beaters beaten unbeaten

beauty beautiful beautifully

big bigger biggest bigness

bright brighter brightest brightness

build builder builders builds building buildings buildable unbuildable rebuild rebuilt rebuilding

call recalled called calling caller callers recall recalls recalling

care careful cares cared caring uncaring careless carefully carelessly carefulness carelessness

complete incomplete completed completes completely incompletely completing completion

compute computer computers computes computed computing

confuse confusion confused confuses confusing

correct incorrect corrects corrected correcting correction corrections correctly incorrectly correctness

crash crashes crashed crashing

danger dangerous dangerously

dark darker darkest darkly darkness

decide decision decisions decides decided deciding indecision undecided

discuss discusses discussed discussing discussion

easy easier easiest easily uneasy

edit editor edits edited editing editors edition editions reedit reedits reedited reediting

elevate elevated elevates elevating elevator elevators

employ employees employs employed employing unemployed employee employment unemployment employable unemployable employer employers

enjoy enjoyment enjoys enjoyed enjoying enjoyable

except exception exceptions exceptional unexceptional

excite excitement excites excited exciting excitable unexciting

expect expects expected expecting unexpected expectation expectations

explode explosion exploded unexploded explodes exploding explosions

fast faster fastest

fill filled fills filling refill refilled refills refilling

float floats floated floating

fry fries fried frying refried

friend friendly friends friendliness friendlier friendliest unfriendly unfriendlier unfriendliest

fright frighten frightened frightening frightful

fun funny funnier funniest

govern governor governs governed governing governors government governable ungovernable

grab grabs grabbed grabbing

happy happiness happier happiest unhappiness unhappiest unhappier unhappy

hard harder hardest hardness

health healthy healthier healthiest healthiness healthful unhealthy unhealthier unhealthiest

heavy heavier heaviest heaviness

help helpless helper helpers helpful helps helped helping helpfully helpfulness helplessly helplessness

hide hides hiding hid hidden

invent inventions inventor invents inventors invented inventing reinvent invention

invest investment investing invests invested investor investors reinvest

library libraries librarian librarians

locate location located locating locations dislocate dislocated relocate relocates relocated relocating relocation dislocation

magic magical magician magicians

marry married marries marrying remarry remarried unmarried

mature immature immaturely

music musical musician musicians

nation nations national nationally

place replace placed places placing replaced replaces replacing placement replacement replacements

poison poisons poisoned poisoning poisonous

probable improbable probably

protect protection protects protected protecting protector protectors unprotected

rain rains rained raining rainy rainier rainiest

ready readiness unready

real really unreal

right rights rightful rightfully

sad sadder saddest sadness sadly

sail sails sailed sailing sailor sailors

science scientist scientists scientific

sense sensible sensibly sensed senses sensing sensor sensors

skate skated skates skating skater skaters

small smaller smallest smallness

stop stopped stops stopping stopper stoppers unstoppable

squirt squirts squirted squirting

swim swims swimming swimmer swimmers

teach teacher teaches teaching teachers reteach reteaches reteaching

thin thinner thinnest thinness thinly

treat treatment treats treated treating treatments treatable untreatable

use used using uses useful usefully useless uselessly usefulness uselessness reused unused

vacate vacates vacated vacating vacation vacations

want wants wanted wanting

wash washable washes washed washing unwashable unwashed washer washers rewash rewashes rewashed rewashing

watch watches watched watching watchful unwatched

weigh weightless weight weightlessness weighs weighed weighing weighty

win wins winning winner winners

write writing writes writer writers rewrite rewrites rewriting written unwritten rewritten

Suffixes and Spelling Changes

These words can be spelled by combining root words from the word wall with the prefixes and suffixes taught. Spelling changes are also reviewed.

es addresses countries crashes discusses fries libraries lunches marries rewashes teaches washes watches

ed acted addressed agreed appeared called cared completed computed confused corrected crashed decided disagreed disappeared discussed dislocated displaced edited elevated employed enjoyed excited expected exploded filled floated fried frightened governed grabbed helped invented invested located married placed poisoned protected rained reacted reappeared recalled reedited refilled refried reinvented relocated remarried replaced reused rewashed sailed sensed skated squirted stopped treated unemployed unexpected unexploded unmarried unused unwashed used wanted washed watched weighed vacated

ing acting addressing agreeing appearing beating building buildings calling caring correcting completing computing confusing crashing deciding disagreeing disappearing discussing editing elevating employing enjoying exciting expecting exploding filling floating frying frightening governing grabbing helping hiding inventing reinventing investing locating marrying remarrying placing replacing poisoning protecting raining reappearing rebuilding recalling reediting relocating replacing reteaching rewashing rewriting sailing sensing skating squirting stopping swimming teaching treating uncaring unexciting using vacating wanting washing watching weighing winning writing

en beaten broken frighten frightened frightening hidden rewritten sadden written unbeaten unwritten

al exceptional exceptionally magical magically musical musically national nationally unexceptional

y rainy healthy weighty

er bigger brighter darker easier faster friendlier unfriendlier funnier happier unhappier unhealthier harder healthier unhealthier heavier sadder smaller thinner

est biggest brightest darkest easiest fastest friendliest unfriendliest funniest happiest unhappiest unhealthiest hardest healthiest unhealthiest heaviest saddest smallest thinnest

ful beautiful beautifully frightful careful carefully carefulness healthful unhealthful helpful unhelpful helpfully rightful rightfully useful usefully usefulness watchful

less careless carelessly carelessness correctness helpless helplessly useless uselessly uselessness weightless weightlessness

able agreeable buildable confusable dependable disagreeable employable enjoyable excitable governable ungovernable treatable washable unbuildable undependable unemployable unenjoyable ungovernable unstoppable untreatable unwashable washable

ible sensible terrible

ous dangerous dangerously poisonous

ic athletic fantastic scientific

136

ly carefully carelessly completely correctly dangerously darkly easily exceptionally friendly unfriendly helpfully helplessly immaturely impossible incorrectly incompletely magically musically maturely nationally possibly probably really sadly sensibly thinly usefully uselessly

ment agreement agreements disagreement disagreements employment enjoyment excitement government governments investment investments placement placements replacement replacements treatment treatments unemployment

ness bigness brightness carefulness carelessness darkness friendliness happiness hardness healthiness heaviness readiness sadness smallness thinness unhappiness usefulness uselessness weightlessness

tion action actions completion correction corrections dislocation edition editions exception exceptions exceptional expectation expectations invention inventions location locations protection reaction reactions relocation unexceptional vacation vacations

sion confusion decision decisions discussion discussions explosion explosions indecision

Suffixes Indicating Person or Thing

er beaters builder builders caller callers computer computers employer employers helper helpers skater skaters stopper stoppers swimmer swimmers teacher teachers washer washers winner winners writer writers

or actor actors editor editors elevator elevators governor governors inventor inventors investor investors protector protectors reactor reactors sailor sailors sensor sensors

ian librarian librarians musician musicians magician magicians

ee employee employees

ist scientist scientists

Prefixes

These words can be spelled by combining root words from the word wall with prefixes and suffixes taught.

re (back or again) react reaction reactions reactor reactors reacts reacted reappear reappeared reappearing reappears rebuild rebuilds rebuilding recall recalling recalled recalls reedit reedits reedited reediting refill refills refilled refilling refried reinvent reinvented reinvest relocate relocated relocates relocating relocation remarried remarry replace replaced replacement replacements replaces replacing reteach reteaches reteaching reuse reused reuses reusing rewash rewashes rewashed rewashing rewrite rewrites rewriting rewritten

un (not or opposite) unbeaten unbuildable uncaring uneasy unemployable unemployed unemployment unexceptional unexciting unexpected unexploded unfriendlier unfriendliest unfriendly ungovernable unhappier unhappiest unhappiness unhappy unhealthier unhealthiest unhealthy unmarried unprotected unready unreal unstoppable untreatable unused unwashable unwashed unwatched unwritten

im/in (not or opposite) immature immaturely impossible impossibly improbable incomplete incompletely incorrect incorrectly indecision

dis (opposite) disagree disagreeable disagreement disagreements disappear disappeared disappearing disappears dislocate dislocated dislocating displaced

Compounds and Contractions

These compounds and contractions can be spelled by using compounds, contractions, and other words on the word wall.

compounds anybody anyone anyplace anything anywhere everybody everyone everything everywhere somebody someone someplace something somewhere

contractions aren't couldn't don't doesn't haven't shouldn't they're wasn't weren't won't wouldn't

WORDO

WORDO is a variation of the ever-popular Bingo game. Students love it and don't even realize they are getting lots of practice reading and writing words. All you need to play WORDO are some sheets of paper on which 25 blocks have been drawn and some small pieces of paper or objects to cover words as they fill in the blocks. You can make your own WORDO sheets or copy the reproducible WORDO sheet on page 139.

You can use WORDO to review the word wall words or to practice extension words. For each WORDO game, choose 24 words. Then, tell the student the word and have them watch while you write it on an index card. They then choose the block on their sheet where they choose to put it. When all 24 words are called out, everyone should have the same 24 words on their sheets—but in different places.

To play the game, the caller shuffles the index cards and calls out words one at a time. Students chant the spelling of the word and then cover the word on their WORDO sheet. The first person to cover a row of words in any direction wins WORDO. The winner reads the words covered to be sure that these words were called. Then, check to see that all words in the winning row were spelled correctly. (If a student has misspelled a word in the winning row, he cannot win and play continues.) When you have a winner, everyone can clear their sheets and play again.

WORDO can be used to review word wall words or to help students focus on extension words. Students pay more attention to the prefix and suffix patterns if you call words that fit a few of the patterns. From the extension lists, you could choose 24 words that have the suffix **ful** or **less**, 24 words that have the "people or things that do" suffixes—**er**, **or**, **ee**, **ian**, **ist**, or 24 words that begin with the prefix **re**. WORDO can help students develop fluency with the key words on the word wall and with their ability to combine roots, prefixes, and suffixes to spell hundreds of other words.

138

WORDO

W	O	R	D	O
		FREE		

Be a Mind Reader

Be a Mind Reader is a favorite word wall review activity. In this game, the teacher thinks of a word on the word wall and then gives five clues to that word. Choose a word and write it on a scrap of paper, but do not let the students see which word you have written. Have students number their papers from one to five, and tell them that you are going to see who can read your mind and figure out which of the word wall words you have written on your paper. Tell them you will give them five clues. By the fifth clue, everyone should guess the word, but if they read your mind they might get it before the fifth clue.

For your first clue, try to tell the students something that will narrow down their choices to words which begin with one to three letters. ("It is a word that begins with **a**, **b**, or **c**.") If you don't have many words on the word wall, you can say, "It's one of our word wall words," for your first clue. Clues may include any features of the word you want the students to notice ("It has more than two letters." "It has less than four letters." "It has an **e**." "It does not have a **t**."). Each succeeding clue should narrow down what the word can be until by clue five, there is only one possible word. As you give each clue, students write the word they believe the chosen word to be next to each number. If a new clue fits the word a student has written for a previous clue, the student writes that word again by the next number. When you give clue five, try to have narrowed it down to only two choices. After you have given the fifth and final clue, show the students the word you wrote on your scratch paper and say, "I know you all have the word next to number five, but who has it next to number four? Three? Two? One?" Usually, someone will have guessed it on the first or second clue. Express amazement that they "read your mind"! Here are a few examples to get you started. You can do this activity with any of the word wall words.

1. It's one of the word wall words.

2. It begins with an **h**.

3. It ends with a suffix.

4. The root word has a spelling change.

5. The root word is **heavy**. (**heavier**)

---

1. It's a word wall word that begins with **w**.

2. It does not have a suffix.

3. It has four letters.

4. It has an **e** in it.

5. What _____ you doing? (**were**)

---

1. It's one of the word wall words that begins with a prefix.

2. The prefix is **re**.

3. It does not have a **d**.

4. It ends with the suffix **ed**.

5. The toys had a dangerous defect and had to be _____. (**recalled**)

---

1. This word ends in a suffix which indicates a person or people who do things.

2. This is not a plural word.

3. This word begins with **s**.

4. This word has six letters.

5. This word ends with **or**. (**sailor**)

Making Words Take-Home Sheet

Prefixes and Suffixes
Total Word List

able	band	can	cruel	don't	except
ace	barn	cape	cry	donut	excite
act	bat	car	cuds	dot	excitement
acting	bay	care	cue	down	exit
action	beat	careful	cure	drag	expect
ad	beaten	cash	customer	drain	expected
address	beautiful	cast	dad	dream	explosion
addresses	bed	cat	Dan	dress	extinct
after	bee	cattle	danger	dressed	eyes
again	beg	cent	dangerous	drill	fact
agree	belt	cheat	dare	drip	fan
agreed	Ben	cheater	dared	dune	fantastic
aim	Bess	claim	dark	each	far
air	best	clam	darkness	ear	fast
all	bet	clap	date	early	faster
also	big	clear	Dean	earth	fat
an	biggest	cleared	dear	easier	fear
and	birth	clue	decision	easiest	feast
ant	bit	coat	deed	east	fed
any	bite	coats	deeds	eat	fee
anybody	body	come	den	eaten	felt
anywhere	bond	compete	dent	eats	fight
ape	bone	complete	depend	Ed	file
appear	born	computers	dependable	edit	fill
are	boss	concert	did	editor	filled
around	boy	confusion	die	eight	fin
as	brain	cool	diet	elevator	find
ash	bran	core	dine	employ	fine
ashes	bride	corn	dined	employees	fire
ask	bright	corner	dirt	end	fired
asked	brightly	correct	disagree	enemy	fit
at	broke	count	disappear	enjoy	float
ate	broken	countries	discuss	enjoyment	floated
athletic	build	country	discussion	erased	fly
baby	builder	county	do	even	fold
bad	but	cousin	does	event	Fred
bag	call	crash	doesn't	ever	free
bail	caller	crashes	Don	every	fried
ban	calm	cries	done	everyone	friend

142

© Carson-Dellosa CD-2413

friendly	help	lap	mature	nod	race
fright	helpless	late	meal	none	rag
frighten	hen	later	mean	noon	rail
fry	hens	law	meaner	noose	rain
fuel	her	lay	meat	nose	rained
fun	here	layer	men	not	rainy
funnier	hid	lead	mess	nut	rake
gain	hidden	leader	mice	oats	rally
garden	hide	left	might	oil	ran
get	hire	lens	mile	old	rare
girl	hit	lenses	miles	on	rash
go	hive	lent	mole	once	rat
goes	home	less	money	one	rate
gone	hound	lessen	monkey	onion	Ray
govern	ice	let	monkeys	or	reach
governors	iciest	librarian	more	our	read
grab	idea	lie	music	oven	readiness
grabbed	if	life	musical	over	real
grad	immature	lift	my	pace	really
grade	impossible	light	nail	pal	rear
greed	in	line	name	pansies	rebuild
grin	incomplete	lion	nation	pencil	recall
grit	incorrect	lit	national	pet	recalled
ground	insect	load	near	pile	red
had	inside	lobby	neat	pin	ref
hair	into	location	Ned	pit	refill
happen	invent	loop	need	place	refilled
happiness	inventions	loose	needed	play	relay
hard	invest	loosen	needle	points	relit
hardest	investment	loss	nest	poison	rename
hat	Ira	lotion	net	poisonous	rent
hate	is	lunch	never	pole	replace
have	it	lunches	new	ponies	retire
heal	jet	magic	newer	pool	rib
health	joy	magicians	news	possible	rid
healthy	Kate	mail	next	probably	ride
hear	Ken	main	nice	protect	rig
heart	key	mall	nicest	protection	right
heat	keys	man	night	quiet	ring
heavier	land	married	nine	quit	rip
heel	landed	mate	nip	quite	ripe

ripen	sent	soon	Ted	tries	when
ripped	set	sooner	tell	trip	where
rise	shade	sore	ten	trot	wig
Rob	shape	sound	tennis	try	win
Ron	share	sour	tent	tune	wing
rope	sheep	spear	terrible	tuned	wings
rose	sheet	spell	test	turn	winners
rot	shell	spider	the	twig	winter
rotten	ship	spies	their	twin	wire
round	shot	spin	then	Ty	wiring
Roy	should	spit	there	unbeaten	wise
royal	shouldn't	spoon	they	uncle	wiser
rude	side	sport	they're	undo	with
ruin	sign	spot	thin	unexpected	won't
rule	simple	spy	thing	union	would
run	sing	squirt	thinner	unsold	wouldn't
sad	sip	squirted	three	us	write
sadness	sipped	stare	tie	use	writing
said	sit	steal	tied	used	written
sail	skate	sting	time	vacations	yarn
sailor	skater	stopping	timer	vent	year
sale	sky	store	tin	very	yet
Sam	slam	suds	tiniest	vest	your
sand	sleep	sue	tip	vet	
sat	sleepy	sun	tire	visit	
saw	small	sweet	tired	vote	
scare	smallest	swim	tiring	voter	
scat	smell	swimming	title	want	
scientist	smile	swing	toad	wanted	
score	snake	table	told	was	
seal	sneak	taco	tool	wash	
seat	snip	tail	top	washable	
second	snoop	take	torn	watch	
see	snore	tall	town	watching	
seed	soil	tame	toy	weight	
seeds	solar	tan	trade	weightless	
seep	sold	teach	travel	went	
sell	some	teacher	treat	were	
send	something	team	treatment	whale	
sense	son	tear	tree	what	
sensible	song	tears	tried	wheel	

Take-Home Word Wall
Lesson 5

A a	G g	R r
addresses are	H h	
		S s
B b	I i	
C c crashes		
	J j	T t
	K k	
D d	L l lunches	
		U u
	M m monkeys	
		V v
E e	N n	W w
	O o	
F f	P p	
	Q q	X x Y y Z z

Take-Home Word Wall
Lesson 10

A a	G g	R r
addresses		
are	H h	
		S s
B b		stopping
	I i	swimming
C c		
crashes		T t
	J j	
	K k	
D d	L l	
	lunches	U u
	M m	
	monkeys	V v
E e		
	N n	W w
		watching
	O o	what
		writing
F f	P p	
	Q q	X x Y y Z z

Take-Home Word Wall
Lesson 15

A a

addresses
are

B b

C c

crashes

D d

E e

F f

floated

G g

grabbed

H h

I i

lunches

J j

monkeys

K k

L l

M m

N n

O o

P p

Q q

R r

S s

stopping
swimming
squirted

T t

U u

used

V v

W w

watching
what
writing
wanted

X x   **Y y**   **Z z**

A a

addresses
are

B b

C c

crashes
country
countries

D d

E e

F f

floated
fried

G g

grabbed

H h

I i

J j

K k

L l

lunches

M m

monkeys
married

N n

O o

our

P p

Q q

R r

S s

stopping
swimming
squirted

T t

U u

used

V v

W w

watching
what
writing
wanted

X x   Y y   Z z

Take-Home Word Wall
Lesson 25

A a
addresses
are

B b
broken

C c
crashes
country
countries

D d

E e

F f
floated
fried
frighten

G g
grabbed

H h
hidden

I i

J j

K k

L l
lunches

M m
monkeys
married

N n

O o
our

P p

Q q

R r

S s
stopping
swimming
squirted

T t

U u
used

V v

W w
watching
what
writing
wanted
went
written

X x   Y y   Z z

Take-Home Word Wall
Lesson 30

A a
addresses
are

B b
broken

C c
crashes
country
countries

D d

E e

F f
floated
fried
frighten

G g
grabbed

H h
hidden
healthy

I i

J j

K k

L l
lunches

M m
monkeys
married
musical

N n
national

O o
our

P p

Q q

R r
rainy

S s
stopping
swimming
squirted

T t
they

U u
used

V v

W w
watching
what
writing
wanted
went
written

X x   **Y y**   **Z z**

Take-Home Word Wall
Lesson 35

A a
addresses
are
anybody
anywhere

B b
broken

C c
crashes
country
countries

D d

E e
everyone

F f
floated
fried
frighten

G g
grabbed

H h
hidden
healthy

I i

J j

K k

L l
lunches

M m
monkeys
married
musical

N n
national

O o
our

P p

Q q

R r
rainy

S s
stopping
swimming
squirted
something

T t
they

U u
used

V v

W w
watching
what
writing
wanted
went
written
were

X x   **Y y**   **Z z**

Take-Home Word Wall
Lesson 40

A a
addresses
are
anybody
anywhere

B b
broken

C c
crashes
country
countries

D d
don't
doesn't

E e
everyone

F f
floated
fried
frighten

G g
grabbed

H h
hidden
healthy

I i

J j

K k

L l
lunches

M m
monkeys
married
musical

N n
national

O o
our

P p

Q q

R r
rainy

S s
stopping
swimming
squirted
something
shouldn't

T t
they
they're

U u
used

V v

W w
watching
what
writing
wanted
went
written
were

wouldn't

X x   Y y   Z z

Take-Home Word Wall
Lesson 45

A a
addresses
are
anybody
anywhere

B b
broken

C c
crashes
country
countries

D d
don't
doesn't

E e
everyone
easiest

F f
floated
fried
frighten
faster

G g
grabbed

H h
hidden   heavier
healthy
hardest
have

I i

J j

K k

L l
lunches

M m
monkeys
married
musical

N n
national

O o
our

P p

Q q

R r
rainy

S s
stopping
swimming
squirted
something
shouldn't

T t
they
they're

U u
used

V v

W w
watching   wouldn't
what
writing
wanted
went
written
were

X x   Y y   Z z

Take-Home Word Wall
Lesson 50

A a
addresses
are
anybody
anywhere

B b
broken
biggest

C c
crashes
country
countries

D d
don't
doesn't

E e
everyone
easiest

F f
funnier

floated
fried
frighten
faster

G g
grabbed

H h
hidden   heavier
healthy
hardest
have

I i

J j

K k

L l
lunches

M m
monkeys
married
musical

N n
national

O o
our

P p

Q q

R r
rainy

S s
stopping
swimming
squirted
something
shouldn't
smallest

T t
they
they're
their
thinner

U u
used

V v

W w
watching   wouldn't
what
writing
wanted
went
written
were

X x   Y y   Z z

Take-Home Word Wall
Lesson 55

A a
addresses
are
anybody
anywhere

B b
broken
biggest

C c
crashes
country
countries
computers

D d
don't
doesn't

E e
everyone
easiest

F f
floated   funnier
fried
frighten
faster

G g
grabbed

H h
hidden   heavier
healthy
hardest
have

I i

J j

K k

L l
lunches

M m
monkeys
married
musical

N n
national

O o
our

P p

Q q

R r
rainy

S s
stopping   skater
swimming
squirted
something
shouldn't
smallest

T t
they   teacher
they're   there
their
thinner

U u
used

V v

W w
watching   wouldn't
what   winners
writing
wanted
went
written
were

X x   **Y y**   **Z z**

Take-Home Word Wall
Lesson 60

A a
addresses   **also**
are
anybody
anywhere

B b
broken
biggest

C c
crashes
country
countries
computers

D d
don't
doesn't

E e
everyone
easiest
editor
elevator

F f
floated   funnier
fried
frighten
faster

G g
grabbed   **governors**

H h
hidden   heavier
healthy
hardest
have

I i

J j

K k

L l
lunches

M m
monkeys
married
musical

N n
national

O o
our

P p

Q q

R r
rainy

S s
stopping   skater
swimming   **sailor**
squirted
something
shouldn't
smallest

T t
they   teacher
they're   there
their
thinner

U u
used

V v

W w
watching   wouldn't
what   winners
writing
wanted
went
written
were

X x   Y y   Z z

156

Take-Home Word Wall
Lesson 65

A a
addresses   also
are
anybody
anywhere

B b
broken
biggest
brightly

C c
crashes
country
countries
computers

D d
don't
doesn't

E e
everyone
easiest
editor
elevator

F f
floated   funnier
fried   friendly
frighten
faster

G g
grabbed   governors

H h
hidden   heavier
healthy
hardest
have

I i

J j

K k

L l
lunches

M m
monkeys
married
musical

N n
national

O o
our

P p
probably

Q q

R r
rainy
really
right

S s
stopping   skater
swimming   sailor
squirted
something
shouldn't
smallest

T t
they   teacher
they're   there
their
thinner

U u
used

V v

W w
watching   wouldn't
what   winners
writing
wanted
went
written
were

X x   Y y   Z z

A a

addresses   also
are
anybody
anywhere

B b   beautiful

broken
biggest
brightly

C c   careful

crashes
country
countries
computers

D d

don't
doesn't

E e

everyone
easiest
editor
elevator

F f

floated   funnier
fried   friendly
frighten
faster

G g

grabbed   governors

H h

hidden   heavier
healthy   helpless
hardest
have

I i

J j

K k

L l

lunches

M m

monkeys
married
musical

N n

national

O o

our

P p

probably

Q q

R r

rainy
really
right

S s

stopping   skater
swimming   sailor
squirted
something
shouldn't
smallest

T t

they   teacher
they're   there
their
thinner

U u

used

V v

W w

watching   wouldn't
what   winners
writing   weightless
wanted   with
went
written
were

X x   Y y   Z z

Take-Home Word Wall
Lesson 75

A a
addresses   also
are
anybody
anywhere

B b
broken   beautiful
biggest
brightly

C c
crashes   careful
country
countries
computers

D d
don't
doesn't
darkness

E e
everyone
easiest
editor
elevator

F f
floated   funnier
fried   friendly
frighten
faster

G g
grabbed   governors

H h
hidden   heavier
healthy   helpless
hardest   happiness
have

I i

J j

K k

L l
lunches

M m
monkeys
married
musical

N n
national

O o
our

P p
probably

Q q

R r
rainy
really
right
readiness

S s
stopping   skater
swimming   sailor
squirted   sadness
something   said
shouldn't
smallest

T t
they   teacher
they're   there
their
thinner

U u
used

V v

W w
watching   wouldn't
what   winners
writing   weightless
wanted   with
went
written
were

X x   Y y   Z z

Take-Home Word Wall
Lesson 80

A a
addresses   also
are
anybody
anywhere

B b
broken   beautiful
biggest   **builder**
brightly

C c
crashes   careful
country
countries
computers

D d
don't
doesn't
darkness

E e
everyone
easiest
editor
elevator

F f
floated   funnier
fried   friendly
frighten
faster

G g
grabbed   governors

H h
hidden   heavier
healthy   helpless
hardest   happiness
have

I i

J j

K k

L l
lunches

M m
monkeys
married
musical

N n
national

O o
our

P p
probably

Q q

R r
rainy   **rebuild**
really   **refilled**
right   **recalled**
readiness   **replace**

S s
stopping   skater
swimming   sailor
squirted   sadness
something   said
shouldn't
smallest

T t
they   teacher
they're   there
their
thinner

U u
used

V v

W w
watching   wouldn't
what   winners
writing   weightless
wanted   with
went
written
were

X x   Y y   Z z

Take-Home Word Wall
Lesson 85

A a
addresses   also
are
anybody
anywhere

B b
broken   beautiful
biggest   builder
brightly

C c
crashes   careful
country
countries
computers

D d
don't
doesn't
darkness
disagree
disappear

E e
everyone
easiest
editor
elevator
except

F f
floated   funnier
fried   friendly
frighten
faster

G g
grabbed   governors

H h
hidden   heavier
healthy   helpless
hardest   happiness
have

I i

J j

K k

L l
lunches

M m
monkeys
married
musical

N n
national

O o
our

P p
probably

Q q

R r
rainy   rebuild
really   refilled
right   recalled
readiness   replace

S s
stopping   skater
swimming   sailor
squirted   sadness
something   said
shouldn't
smallest

T t
they   teacher
they're   there
their
thinner

U u
used   unexpected
unbeaten

V v

W w
watching   wouldn't
what   winners
writing   weightless
wanted   with
went
written
were

X x   Y y   Z z

Take-Home Word Wall
Lesson 90

A a
addresses   also
are
anybody
anywhere

B b
broken   beautiful
biggest   builder
brightly

C c
crashes   careful
country
countries
computers

D d
don't
doesn't
darkness
disagree
disappear

E e
everyone
easiest
editor
elevator
except

F f
floated   funnier
fried   friendly
frighten
faster

G g
grabbed   governors

H h
hidden   heavier
healthy   helpless
hardest   happiness
have

I i
immature   into
impossible
incorrect
incomplete

J j

K k

L l
lunches

M m
monkeys
married
musical

N n
national

O o
our

P p
probably

Q q

R r
rainy   rebuild
really   refilled
right   recalled
readiness   replace

S s
stopping   skater
swimming   sailor
squirted   sadness
something   said
shouldn't
smallest

T t
they   teacher
they're   there
their
thinner

U u
used   unexpected
unbeaten

V v

W w
watching   wouldn't
what   winners
writing   weightless
wanted   with
went
written
were

X x   Y y   Z z

Take-Home Word Wall
Lesson 95

A a
addresses   also
are   **again**
anybody
anywhere

B b
broken   beautiful
biggest   builder
brightly

C c
crashes   careful
country
countries
computers

D d
don't
doesn't
darkness
disagree
disappear

E e
everyone
easiest
editor
elevator
except
employees

F f
floated   funnier
fried   friendly
frighten
faster

G g
grabbed   governors

H h
hidden   heavier
healthy   helpless
hardest   happiness
have

I i
immature   into
impossible
incorrect
incomplete

J j

K k

L l
lunches
librarian

M m
monkeys   **magicians**
married
musical

N n
national

O o
our

P p
probably

Q q

R r
rainy   rebuild
really   refilled
right   recalled
readiness   replace

S s
stopping   skater
swimming   sailor
squirted   sadness
something   said
shouldn't   **scientist**
smallest

T t
they   teacher
they're   there
their
thinner

U u
used   unexpected
unbeaten

V v

W w
watching   wouldn't
what   winners
writing   weightless
wanted   with
went
written
were

X x   Y y   Z z

© Carson-Dellosa CD-2413

163

Take-Home Word Wall
Lesson 100

A a
addresses   also
are   again
anybody   action
anywhere

B b
broken   beautiful
biggest   builder
brightly

C c
crashes   careful
country
countries
computers

D d
don't
doesn't
darkness
disagree
disappear

E e
everyone
easiest
editor
elevator
except
employees

F f
floated   funnier
fried   friendly
frighten
faster

G g
grabbed   governors

H h
hidden   heavier
healthy   helpless
hardest   happiness
have

I i
immature   into
impossible   inventions
incorrect
incomplete

J j

K k

L l
lunches   location
librarian

M m
monkeys   magicians
married
musical

N n
national

O o
our

P p
probably
protection

Q q

R r
rainy   rebuild
really   refilled
right   recalled
readiness   replace

S s
stopping   skater
swimming   sailor
squirted   sadness
something   said
shouldn't   scientist
smallest

T t
they   teacher
they're   there
their
thinner

U u
used   unexpected
unbeaten

V v
vacations

W w
watching   wouldn't
what   winners
writing   weightless
wanted   with
went
written
were

X x   Y y   Z z

Take-Home Word Wall
Lesson 105

A a
addresses   also
are   again
anybody   action
anywhere

B b
broken   beautiful
biggest   builder
brightly

C c
crashes   careful
country   confusion
countries   cousin
computers

D d
don't   decision
doesn't   discussion
darkness
disagree
disappear

E e
everyone   explosion
easiest
editor
elevator
except
employees

F f
floated   funnier
fried   friendly
frighten
faster

G g
grabbed   governors

H h
hidden   heavier
healthy   helpless
hardest   happiness
have

I i
immature   into
impossible   inventions
incorrect
incomplete

J j

K k

L l
lunches   location
librarian

M m
monkeys   magicians
married
musical

N n
national

O o
our

P p
probably
protection

Q q

R r
rainy   rebuild
really   refilled
right   recalled
readiness   replace

S s
stopping   skater
swimming   sailor
squirted   sadness
something   said
shouldn't   scientist
smallest

T t
they   teacher
they're   there
their
thinner

U u
used   unexpected
unbeaten

V v
vacations

W w
watching   wouldn't
what   winners
writing   weightless
wanted   with
went
written
were

X x   Y y   Z z

Take-Home Word Wall
Lesson 110

A a
addresses
are
anybody
anywhere

also
again
action

B b
broken
biggest
brightly

beautiful
builder

C c
crashes
country
countries
computers

careful
confusion
cousin

D d
don't
doesn't
darkness
disagree
disappear

decision
discussion
dependable

E e
everyone
easiest
editor
elevator
except
employees

explosion

F f
floated
fried
frighten
faster

funnier
friendly

G g
grabbed

governors

H h
hidden
healthy
hardest
have

heavier
helpless
happiness

I i
immature
impossible
incorrect
incomplete

into
inventions

J j

K k

L l
lunches
librarian

location

M m
monkeys
married
musical

magicians

N n
national

O o
our

P p
probably
protection

Q q

R r
rainy
really
right
readiness

rebuild
refilled
recalled
replace

S s
stopping
swimming
squirted
something
shouldn't
smallest

skater
sailor
sadness
said
scientist
sensible

T t
they
they're
their
thinner

teacher
there
terrible

U u
used
unbeaten

unexpected

V v
vacations

W w
watching
what
writing
wanted
went
written
were

wouldn't
winners
weightless
with
was
washable

X x   Y y   Z z

Take-Home Word Wall
Lesson 115

A a
addresses also
are again
anybody action
anywhere

B b
broken beautiful
biggest builder
brightly

C c
crashes careful
country confusion
countries cousin
computers

D d
don't decision
doesn't discussion
darkness dependable
disagree
disappear

E e
everyone explosion
easiest enjoyment
editor excitement
elevator
except
employees

F f
floated funnier
fried friendly
frighten
faster

G g
grabbed governors

H h
hidden heavier
healthy helpless
hardest happiness
have

I i
immature into
impossible inventions
incorrect investment
incomplete

J j

K k

L l
lunches location
librarian

M m
monkeys magicians
married
musical

N n
national none

O o
our

P p
probably
protection

Q q

R r
rainy rebuild
really refilled
right recalled
readiness replace

S s
stopping skater
swimming sailor
squirted sadness
something said
shouldn't scientist
smallest sensible

T t
they teacher
they're there
their terrible
thinner treatment

U u
used unexpected
unbeaten

V v
vacations

W w
watching wouldn't
what winners
writing weightless
wanted with
went was
written washable
were

X x Y y Z z

Take-Home Word Wall
Lesson 120

A a
addresses · again
are · action
anybody · around
anywhere · athletic
also

B b
broken · beautiful
biggest · builder
brightly

C c
crashes · careful
country · confusion
countries · cousin
computers

D d
don't · decision
doesn't · discussion
darkness · dependable
disagree · dangerous
disappear

E e
everyone · employees
easiest · explosion
editor · enjoyment
elevator · excitement
except

F f
floated · funnier
fried · friendly
frighten · fantastic
faster

G g
grabbed · governors

H h
hidden · heavier
healthy · helpless
hardest · happiness
have

I i
immature · into
impossible · inventions
incorrect · investment
incomplete

J j

K k

L l
lunches · location
librarian

M m
monkeys · magicians
married
musical

N n
national · none

O o
our

P p
probably · poisonous
protection

Q q

R r
rainy · rebuild
really · refilled
right · recalled
readiness · replace

S s
stopping · skater
swimming · sailor
squirted · sadness
something · said
shouldn't · scientist
smallest · sensible

T t
they · teacher
they're · there
their · terrible
thinner · treatment

U u
used · unexpected
unbeaten

V v
vacations

W w
watching · wouldn't
what · winners
writing · weightless
wanted · with
went · was
written · washable
were

X x   Y y   Z z

Reproducible Word Strips

Lesson 1 | **Lesson 2** | **Lesson 3** | **Lesson 4**

Lesson 1: y s n m k o e

Lesson 2: s n l h c u e

Lesson 3: s s r h c e a

Lesson 4: s s s r d d e e a

© Carson-Dellosa CD-2413

Lesson 6	Lesson 7	Lesson 8	Lesson 9
a i c g h n t w	i i g n r t w	i i g m n s w	i o g n p s t

Reproducible Word Strips

Lesson 11	Lesson 12	Lesson 13	Lesson 14
w	r	t	t
t	g	s	l
n	d	r	f
d	b	q	d
e	b	d	o
a	e	u	e
a	a	i	a
		e	

Lesson 16	Lesson 17	Lesson 18	Lesson 19
o u c n r t y	e i o u c n r t s	e i d f r	a e i d m r r

Reproducible Word Strips

Lesson 21	Lesson 22	Lesson 23	Lesson 24
t	r	n	w
r	n	h	t
h	k	d	t
g	b	d	r
f	o	i	n
i			i
e	e	e	e

Lesson 26 **Lesson 27** **Lesson 28** **Lesson 29**

Lesson 26	Lesson 27	Lesson 28	Lesson 29
y	y	s	t
t	r	m	n
l	n	l	n
h	i	c	l
h	t	u	o
e	a	i	i
a		a	a
			a

Lesson 31 **Lesson 32** **Lesson 33** **Lesson 34**

Lesson 31	Lesson 32	Lesson 33	Lesson 34
t	y	y	y
s	v	y	w
n	r	n	r
m	n	d	n
h	o	b	h
g	e	o	e
o	e	a	a
i	e		
e			

Lesson 36   **Lesson 37**   **Lesson 38**   **Lesson 39**

Lesson 36	Lesson 37	Lesson 38	Lesson 39
y	t	w	t
t	s	t	s
r	n	n	n
h	d	l	l
e	o	p	h
e	e	o	p
			o

Reproducible Word Strips

Lesson 41 **Lesson 42** **Lesson 43** **Lesson 44**

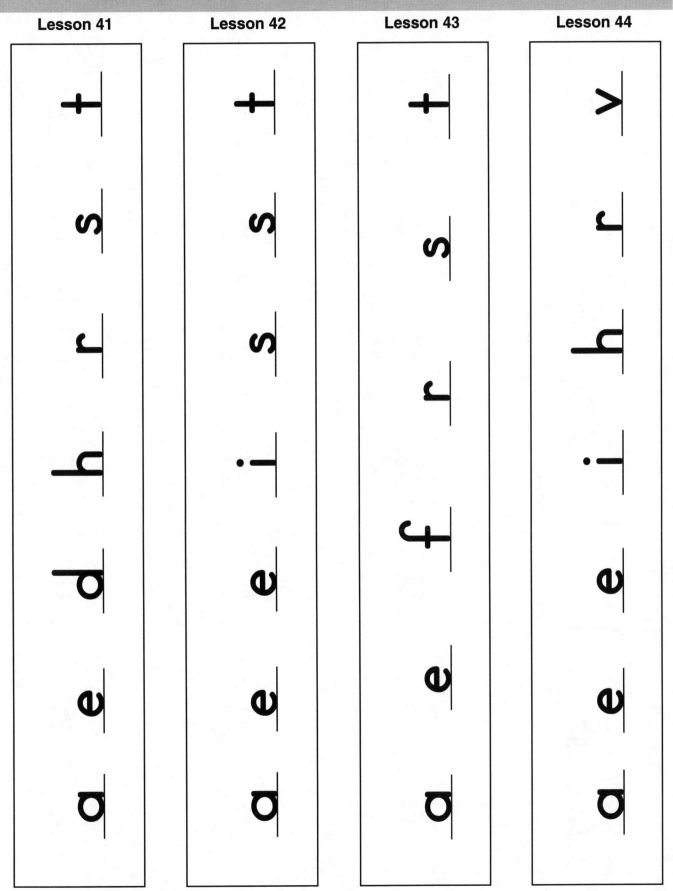

Lesson 41: a e d h r s t

Lesson 42: a e i s s t

Lesson 43: a e f r s t

Lesson 44: a e i h r v

Lesson 46 **Lesson 47** **Lesson 48** **Lesson 49**

Lesson 46	Lesson 47	Lesson 48	Lesson 49
t	t	t	r
s	s	r	n
s	g	n	n
m	g	h	f
l	b	h	u
l	i	i	e
e	e	e	i
a			

Reproducible Word Strips

Lesson 51 | Lesson 52 | Lesson 53 | Lesson 54

Lesson 51: t r h c e a

Lesson 52: t s r p m c u o e

Lesson 53: t s r k e a

Lesson 54: w s r n n i e

Lesson 56

t r d i e

Lesson 57

s r l i a

Lesson 58

v s r r n g o e

Lesson 59

v t r l o e a

Lesson 61   **Lesson 62**   **Lesson 63**   **Lesson 64**

Lesson 61	Lesson 62	Lesson 63	Lesson 64
y	y	y	y
r	r	r	r
t	n	p	l
l	l	l	T
h	f	b	T
g	d	b	e
b	i	o	a
i	e	a	

Lesson 66

a e u c f f l r

Lesson 67

a e i u u b f l t

Lesson 68

e e h l T l p s s

Lesson 69

e e i g h l s s t w

Lesson 71	Lesson 72	Lesson 73	Lesson 74
s	s	s	s
r	s	s	s
n	n	p	r
k	d	p	n
d		n	d
e	e	h	i
a	a	i	e
		e	a
		a	

Lesson 76 | **Lesson 77** | **Lesson 78** | **Lesson 79**

Lesson 76: r l d b u i e

Lesson 77: r l f d i l e e

Lesson 78: r p l c e a

Lesson 79: r l l d c c e a

Reproducible Word Strips

Lesson 81	Lesson 82	Lesson 83	Lesson 84
t	x	s	s
n	t	r	r
n	p	g	p
u	n	d	p
b	d	i	d
e	c	e	i
e	u	e	e
a	e	a	a
	e		a

Lesson 86	Lesson 87	Lesson 88	Lesson 89
s	t	t	t
s	r	r	p
p	m	r	n
m	m	n	m
l	u	c	l
b	i	c	c
o	e	o	o
i	a	i	i
i		e	e
e			e

Reproducible Word Strips

Lesson 91   **Lesson 92**   **Lesson 93**   **Lesson 94**

Lesson 91	Lesson 92	Lesson 93	Lesson 94
r	s	y	t
n	n	s	t
l	m	p	s
b	g	m	s
i	c	l	n
i	i	o	c
a	i	e	i
a	a	e	i
	a	e	e

Reproducible Word Strips

Lesson 96

y t s n n o i i e

Lesson 97

t t r p n c o o i e

Lesson 98

t n l c o o i a

Lesson 99

y t s n c o i a a

Reproducible Word Strips

Lesson 101 **Lesson 102** **Lesson 103** **Lesson 104**

Lesson 101	Lesson 102	Lesson 103	Lesson 104
s	x	s	s
s	s	n	n
n	p	n	d
d	l	f	c
c	o	c	o
u	o	u	o
o	i	o	t
i	e	l	i
i		i	e

Lesson 106   **Lesson 107**   **Lesson 108**   **Lesson 109**

Lesson 111   **Lesson 112**   **Lesson 113**   **Lesson 114**

e e o j m n n t y

a e e m n r t t t

e e e i c m n t t x

e e i m n n s t t v

Lesson 116

i o o o u n p s s

Lesson 117

a e o u d g n r s

Lesson 118

a e i c h h l t t

Lesson 119

a a i c f n s t t